# Deep Creativity

To Krysia,
Here & Now, Baby!
Love & Joy

# deep Creativity

*Inside the Creative Mystery*

Victor Shamas, Ph.D.

FOREWORD BY C. June Maker, Ph.D.

NEW YORK

NASHVILLE • MELBOURNE • VANCOUVER

# Deep Creativity

*Inside the Creative Mystery*

Published in New York, New York, by Morgan James Publishing. Morgan James is a trademark of Morgan James, LLC. www.MorganJamesPublishing.com

The Morgan James Speakers Group can bring authors to your live event. For more information or to book an event visit The Morgan James Speakers Group at www.TheMorganJamesSpeakersGroup.com.

Cover image of the Helix Nebula, taken by the Hubble Space Telescope in 2007, courtesy of NASA

ISBN 9781683505419 paperback
ISBN 9781683505426 eBook
Library of Congress Control Number: 2017905623

**Cover Design by:**
Rachel Lopez
www.r2cdesign.com

**Interior Design by:**
Chris Treccani
www.3dogcreative.net

**Illustrations by:**
Marnie Sharp

In an effort to support local communities, raise awareness and funds, Morgan James Publishing donates a percentage of all book sales for the life of each book to Habitat for Humanity Peninsula and Greater Williamsburg.

Get involved today! Visit
www.MorganJamesBuilds.com

*The role of the artist is to hold up a vision of spiritual reality.*
—Joseph Campbell


*If I create from the heart, nearly everything works; if from the head, almost nothing.*
—Marc Chagall


*Anticipation of joy. The call. To speak of mystery in terms of mystery. Is this not the conscious and unconscious goal of the compelling urge to create?*
—Wassily Kandinsky


*Art is a form of religion, minus the Ten Commandment business, which is sociological. Art is a form of supremely delicate awareness and atonement— meaning at oneness, the state of being in one with the object. But is the great atonement in delight?—for I can never look at art save as a form of delight.*
—D. H. Lawrence

*We are generally afraid to become that which we can glimpse in our most perfect moments under conditions of greatest courage. Only people who have the arrogance of creativity dare to reach for the highest possibilities.*
—Abraham Maslow

*You cannot govern the creative impulse; all you can do is eliminate obstacles and smooth the way for it.*
—Kimon Nicolaides

*Every act of creation is first of all an act of destruction.*
—Pablo Picasso

*The task of the creative individual, then, is to unite, to find harmony in the midst of discord, and love where enmity prevails. Like the mystic, the creator perceives a world of myriad parts that ultimately mold into one.*
—Marilyn Whiteside

*And now let's lower our voice and be a bit wary! For we want to enter the realm of creativity. This space does not permit a direct approach. It does not respond to concrete demands. It does not yet know the structure, it knows neither name nor number. It does not want to yield to anything, it does not heed commends. It is the space of creative readiness and is a sanctuary.*
—Mary Wigman

*To the unfathomable creative power*
*that is your birthright*

# CONTENTS

# FOREWORD

*"The world we have created is a product of our thinking; it cannot be changed without changing our thinking."*
—Albert Einstein

When I was eight years old, I had a significant dream that has been the inspiration for my life's work as a researcher and educator. In this dream, I saw adults putting children in boxes. They put them in boxes of all sizes and shapes and of all sorts of pretty colors; and even tied beautiful bows around them. But they were still boxes! The children hated being in these boxes, and as a child, I could see the children inside the boxes, so I went around from adult to adult, tugging on their coattails or the hems of their dresses, and telling them they were hurting the children, and to please let them out of the boxes. I became very frustrated, and was sobbing and pleading with the adults. But no one listened.

I awoke still highly disturbed at what I had seen, also knowing that's how I often felt in school and in my church. I told my mother about the dream, and in her infinite wisdom, she said, "When you get older, people will listen." Now, as a seasoned researcher and writer, I can say that she was right; and I have been able to develop teaching methods and curricula as well as create unique assessments for children and adolescents that are used around the world. I have also gathered evidence of the effectiveness of these methods.

Starting with my first book, *Curriculum Development and Teaching Strategies for Gifted Learners*, I have advocated removing the barriers and limitations of our thinking about others and their potential: removing the boxes we have built around them by the teaching methods we have used, but most of all by our own thinking about their potential. I was the first to write about the **abilities** of people with certain limiting conditions such as blindness, deafness, and mobility limitations; and in all my books about teaching, advocated the development of teacher attitudes and learning environments characterized by openness, acceptance, learner-centeredness, flexibility, and mobility.

From this early emphasis on what many considered a select group of individuals with certain genetic, intellectual, and personality traits, and the research I directed, I came to realize that many more children and adolescents possess the potential to change their thinking, change their worlds, and change themselves, if only their teachers, parents, caregivers, and others in their lives can help them free themselves rather than adding more bars to their prisons. In many of my studies, an observer sits with a group of children, leads them through a series of activities with decreasing amounts of structure, and then watches their process as they create stories, build things, solve puzzles, and compose music. My most exciting years have been spent watching children from many different cultures and environments; and being continually amazed at what I am seeing! They possess within themselves a universe of possibilities.

In my latest attempt to continue and expand these ideas, my research team and I created extensive plans for Centers for Innovation and Creativity for the government of Saudi Arabia, with the idea that they would be built in every region of the country, and would serve everyone in the community, from birth to death, and with no admission fees. Now, one of my main goals is to promote the creation of such centers in every corner of the world!

However, in my 38 years of research and writing, something has been missing. Perhaps part of this was my own limitation: in my attempts to have my work accepted by the educational and scientific community, I followed a fairly conventional path in research methodology, incorporating experimental methods as much as possible, but tweaking them so that I could be true to my overall purposes. When observing children's creativity, my research team and I asked them to describe their creations, but we did not question them closely about their process; and although we carefully documented their enjoyment of the tasks, we did not in all cases ask them about their passion or about what they enjoyed the most. Like most researchers in the field, we focused mainly on the creative product, not ignoring the process of creating, but in some ways dismissing its importance because we did not have acceptable methods for studying it. This focus on process and the emotional component of this process has been a missing element in the research and writing of many, if not most, researchers in the field of creativity.

When Victor Shamas asked me to read his book, *Deep Creativity*, I was tremendously excited. I had read his other three books, and had seen the revolutionary nature of their content as well as the skill and creativity of their author. Now, here was a book related to my own field of study. My thinking and my world could be expanded, and my understanding of ways to help people get out of the boxes placed by others and by themselves could be deepened and extended. That is indeed what happened, and my excitement increased from the moment I began reading until the last word!

Our ordinary and conventional methods for attempting to describe and understand the phenomenon of creativity have been confined largely to those that meet the standards of replicability, validity, and reliability; as seen in the current emphasis on "evidence-based" practices and "quality indicators" for manuscripts, which are now appearing in almost every field of educational and psychological research. But these methods are not sufficient for the study of a phenomenon as complex as creativity; and you will not find these methods prevailing in *Deep Creativity*. You will certainly find a scientific approach, through analysis of the writings of creative individuals and mystics, but you also will find a first-person approach in which these writings are integrated with the author's personal exploration of the creative process. To me, this is unique and potentially revolutionary.

The methods used in *Deep Creativity* lead to extraordinary insights. Victor Shamas challenges basic assumptions about the nature of creativity, including its source and inner workings, the powerful role of passion and other deeply-felt emotions, and the importance of cultivating qualities within ourselves that are accessible to virtually anyone—not just a select few. It shows us that unlocking the mysteries of creativity does not happen by **doing**, but by **being**: being who we really are, letting go of the beliefs and assumptions that hold us back so that we can discover this fundamental truth about ourselves: that we were all born to create!

I am convinced, after reading this book, that in the Centers for Creativity and Innovation I am advocating and in the assessments my colleagues and I have created, if we incorporate the ideas in this book, we can truly remove those boxes I saw in my dream as an 8-year-old child. And perhaps even more importantly, we can see that in each adult, there is a child who has been put in a box and needs to be freed!

C. June Maker, PhD.
Department of Disability and Psychoeducational Studies
University of Arizona
November 5, 2016

# ACKNOWLEDGMENTS

For 30 years, *Deep Creativity* has been a part of my life. From the first moment of revelation to the last round of edits, the making of this book has been a profound adventure. It is the reason why I changed fields from chemistry to psychology at age 30 and moved from the Pacific Northwest to the Arizona desert. Nearly two decades ago, I sat down to write this book, only to discover after several months that I had much more to learn before I could finish what I had started. That realization led me to immerse myself more fully in my own creative process, which gave me the chance to cross paths with artists, mystics, and visionaries who would help inspire *Deep Creativity*.

I could never have completed a project of this magnitude without the help of countless people. Literally, thousands of individuals have contributed to *Deep Creativity* in some way, starting with my parents, David and Sara; brother and sister-in-law, Daniel and Susan; nieces, Jenna, Sarina, and Amiyah; and nephew-in-law Eldon. Their love and support have lifted me up and kept me going every step of the way.

In 1996, I co-founded a network of chanting circles called Global Chant, which has turned out to be an important testing site for the ideas in *Deep Creativity*. These circles have brought many kindred spirits into my life, starting with my beloved partner in Repose, Jhan Kold, and her family. Although I cannot begin to name them all, I would like to single out a few: Deborah Beaumont, Camille

Bonzani, James Counts, Henry Foster, Antonio Gomez, Mark Gouhin, Ellie and Katie Hall, Aryen Hart, Erin Madden, Chuck McDuffie, Wanda Poindexter, Jorge Porrata, Caroline Ragano, David Torre, and Jennifer Treece. There are perhaps five thousand other members of the Global Chant community that are deserving of mention here. I offer my heartfelt thanks to every one of them.

A number of teachers and mentors have been instrumental in my development as a scholar and a person. First and foremost among them are my maternal grandparents, Yomtov and Ines Policar, whose presence I feel on a daily basis, long after their passing. Other dear teachers who are gone but not forgotten include Dr. Adela Allen, Jerry Elarth, Dr. Lee Sechrest, Dr. Fred Tabbutt, and Dr. Byron Youtz. I have had the privilege to learn from so many wonderful individuals at every institution I have attended: Seattle Hebrew Academy, Roosevelt High School, the University of Washington, The Evergreen State College, the University of California at Santa Cruz, and the University of Arizona. Nothing is more precious in my life than the teachers who have inspired me through their wisdom, insight, and compassion.

Seeing *Deep Creativity* in print is a long-term dream of mine, and I want to thank several people who helped make this dream a reality. Besides writing a beautiful foreword, Dr. June Maker has been a loyal friend and supporter who helped introduce *Deep Creativity* to a global audience. Marnie Sharp contributed her graphic design talents and artistic vision to this project. Lynn Wiese opened doors for the publication of *Deep Creativity* and has offered her sage advice as a friend and publicist. The entire team at Morgan James Publishing believed in this vision and helped push the project forward.

At the core of *Deep Creativity* are transcendent emotions such as love, joy, bliss, and ecstasy. I offer my deepest gratitude to the spiritual teachers, friends, students, and other loved ones that have opened my heart to these profound emotions in lasting ways and helped propel me on this extraordinary journey. I would like to honor these wonderful and amazing individuals with the words of one of the first songs I ever wrote: "You are in my heart, living in my heart, always in my heart."

# INTRODUCTION

*"Creativeness contains a secret."*
—Carl Jung

A radical new approach to the study of creativity is taking shape. This approach, called Deep Creativity, involves participation rather than observation. In Deep Creativity, the researcher delves into the creative process the way a frogman dives into the ocean. Following in the footsteps of artists throughout history, the investigator-explorer gains new insights not only into the nature of creativity, but perhaps more importantly, into the most profound mysteries of human existence.

To be honest, the field of Deep Creativity consists of one person right now. Maybe this will change by the time you read my words. But as I write this book, I feel a little like Jeff Clark, the first surfer to attempt riding the 50-foot waves at Mavericks. Located in Half Moon Bay, some 20 miles south of San Francisco, Mavericks features waves that break half a mile off shore onto jagged rocks. For 15 years, Clark surfed Mavericks by himself, unable to entice anyone else to join him at what was then considered more of a navigational hazard than a world-class surfing locale.[1]

My efforts may seem a little less heroic, and I admit that I am not risking life and limb here. But I have chosen to sacrifice my academic reputation and career advancement in order to share Deep Creativity with you. As a psychologist, I know that my academic colleagues look down upon what they call "first-person approaches" to the study of human experience and behavior. Such approaches require crossing the line between researcher and subject. The investigator dares to enter the fray, taking on the role of observer and participant simultaneously. Although modern psychology began with the work of 19th Century introspectionists who did just that, the field quickly rejected their methods in favor of experimental approaches that established a greater degree of separation between scientist and subject.

The problem is that these experimental methods are not very effective at illuminating certain key aspects of human creativity. There is a type of creative experience that differs profoundly from the ordinary waking consciousness of most people. It involves visions and voices, dreams and trance, passion and ecstasy. Scientists who study creativity tend to disregard this type of experience because they do not see it as *replicable*. If they are unable to reproduce an experience with a group of randomly selected research subjects (i.e. college freshmen taking introductory psychology), scientists will give it a wide berth. In fact, they might even dismiss any accounts of such experiences as lacking in validity and reliability—the two cornerstones of scientific acceptability.

Yet the non-ordinary creative experiences that scientists are overlooking have been linked to some of the greatest breakthroughs in art, music, literature, poetry, and science. Moreover, they reveal something remarkable about human beings pertaining not just to our creativity but also to our common origins and undiscovered potential. In disregarding these experiences, the scientific study of creativity has limited itself in ways that hinder its effectiveness.

More precisely, the field has hit a brick wall. Here is all the proof you need that the scientific approach to creativity is not working: In a 2010 article entitled simply "Creativity," noted scholars Beth Hennessey and Teresa Amabile took on the daunting task of reviewing all of the creativity research published in the previous decade.[2] After examining more than 500 journal articles, book chapters, and monographs, these two authors produced an extensive summary that looked at creativity from various perspectives, including the neurological level, the individual, groups, social environments, culture, and overall systems. Their article makes no mention of the creative process as experienced and described by artists. Not one.[3] At a time when research on creativity has exploded, scientists have made little progress in understanding the inner workings of real-world creativity.

When describing the creative process, investigators in this field still cite a 90-year-old theory. In his 1926 book, *The Art of Thought*, Graham Wallas proposed a model of the creative process consisting of the following four stages: preparation, incubation, illumination, and verification.[4] For the record, I do not reject things just because they are old. One look at my clothes closet will confirm this point. The problem I have with Wallas' model is that it merely assigns labels to these stages but fails to shed much light on them—particularly the crucial stages of incubation and illumination. I am reminded of a classic cartoon, depicted here:

*I think you should be more explicit here in Step 2*

I know this all makes me sound anti-science, but I am not. Science offers an elegant method for exploring the natural world. On a daily basis, we can give thanks for the many ways that science has expanded our known universe, opening our minds to everything from quarks and prions to black holes and supernovae. From a practical standpoint, I don't need to tell you how new technologies and advances in public health have enhanced and extended our lives. Granted, some of those technologies may end up destroying human civilization, but let's just assume that the issue has more to do with failures in global leadership than the evils of science.

The reason we need Deep Creativity is that the scientific method is simply not well-suited to the study of the creative process. Some types of experiences can be understood more thoroughly from the inside. One of the great illustrations of this point can be found in the *Electric Kool-Aid Acid Test*, Tom Wolfe's chronicle of author Ken Kesey's experimentation with LSD in the 1960s. Kesey wrote two of the most acclaimed novels of the century, *One Flew over the Cuckoo's Nest* and *Sometimes a Great Notion*, while under the influence of LSD and other psychoactive drugs. His first exposure to LSD came when he volunteered to be a subject in clinical drug trials taking place at the Veterans Hospital in Menlo Park, California. In these trials, participants were given either the drug or placebo and then placed under observation in a closed hospital room.

At various points during the trials, clinicians wearing lab coats and carrying clipboards would enter Kesey's room to test the effects of the drug on specific psychological functions. Wolfe describes an episode in which one of the researchers comes in to check on Kesey's time perception. The clinician instructs Kesey:

> Now when I say "Go," you tell me when you think a minute is up by saying, "Now." Have you got that?
>
> Yeah, he had that. Kesey was soaring on LSD and his sense of time was *wasted*, and thousands of thoughts per second were rapping around between synapses, fractions of a second, so what the hell is a minute—but then one thought stuck in there, held…ma-*li*-cious, *de*-li-cious. He remembered that his pulse

had been running 75 beats a minute every time they took it, so when Dr. Fog says, "Go," Kesey slyly slides his slithering finger onto his pulse and counts up to 75 and says:

"Now!"

Dr. Smog looks at his stop watch. "Amazing!" he says, and walks out of the room.

You said it, bub, but like a lot of other people, you don't even know. [5]

In this scenario, Kesey sees himself and not the clinician as the real researcher. After all, he knows first-hand what it feels like to be tripping on acid. None of the scientists have taken LSD themselves, and so they have no comprehension of the kinds of experiences he could be undergoing. They have no choice but to rely on the verbal reports of their subjects, which in this case proves highly unreliable because of Kesey's inability or unwillingness to attempt an explanation of what he is actually experiencing.

With near-perfect consistency, scientists who study consciousness will choose third-person over first-person approaches, even though their methods leave them in the disadvantaged position of being on the outside looking in. I began my research career in a hypnosis lab and had the good fortune of meeting some of the most influential researchers in that field.[6] At one hypnosis conference, my graduate advisor invited me to join him and some of his colleagues for a happy hour. Suddenly, I found myself sitting at a table surrounded by a *who's who*, if you will, of hypnosis researchers. At one point, just for fun, I asked each of the scientists at the table to describe his or her personal experience with hypnosis. Much to my surprise, none of them had ever been hypnotized. In fact, most of them claimed—with some degree of pride—that they were not "susceptible" to hypnosis. One of them even went so far as to admit that he had never had a mental image of any kind in his entire life!

In our society, a dramatic rift separates first-hand and third-hand ways of knowing, and there is little question as to which approach is considered more acceptable. Physicians administer a treatment to a patient, whereas shamans may undergo the treatment themselves. Churchgoers learn about revelation through scripture, whereas mystics rely on direct experience. And in creativity research, scientists study the creativity of others whereas artists immerse themselves in their own creative process. Clearly, those who adopt first-hand methods are more likely to find themselves on the fringes of society.

Deep Creativity draws upon the direct experiences and reports of artists and mystics alike. Here, I use the term *artist* to refer to anyone who explores the creative process from within. In this regard, Albert Einstein would be considered an artist. So would inventors like Nikola Tesla and Elias Howe. These remarkable men immersed themselves in the process of discovery and then documented their experience with thoroughness and care. Einstein may have revolutionized the way theoretical physicists approach their work as much as he did the science itself.

As for mystics, they attain insight into core mysteries that transcend the human intellect. Their methods, which include contemplation, self-surrender, and intuition, allow them to experience non-ordinary states through which the absolute is revealed to them directly. The artist and mystic are often one and the same, as in the case of poets like Wordsworth and Blake; composers like Wagner and Bach; writers like Hesse and Huxley; or painters like Tobey and Callahan.

In Deep Creativity, art and mysticism collide because the exploration of human creativity leads invariably to a core reality that is both *immanent,* meaning that it abides deep within you, and *transcendent,* meaning that it connects you to something greater than yourself. It turns out that artists and mystics both understand something that the scientists do not. They are able to access realms of experience far richer and more complex than anything scientific methods and instruments can begin to measure.

At one time, I was one of those scientists studying creativity—or at least I tried to be. My doctoral dissertation offered the most direct evidence that had been found up to that point for the existence of unconscious processes in creativity.[7] When I traveled to universities and scientific conferences to present my findings, I was met with much more skepticism than I could have anticipated. To me, the controversy seemed like a tempest in a teapot. Ask anyone who does not have a "Ph.D." after their name if some part of the creative process happens unconsciously, and they will generally reply: "Of course!" When it came time to publish my dissertation findings, I had lost interest in the endeavor, much to my former advisor's chagrin. I wondered why I was trying so hard to convince a small, skeptical audience of something so obvious.

Instead, I decided to explore creativity through direct experience. This decision was my moment of departure. Rather than observing creativity in others, I immersed myself in the creative process as fully as I could. Over the next two decades, my creative output just exploded. During that time, I wrote hundreds of musical compositions, made over 200 videos, authored four books, started a non-profit group that has gone international, developed and taught 25 university courses, organized a global event called WAVE1 that involved approximately one million participants in 40 countries, designed multimedia materials on the neuroscience of addiction, invented a solar water distiller, created an anti-inflammatory lifestyle to lower the risk of chronic illness, and—perhaps most importantly—co-discovered a relaxation technique called Repose[8] that has had positive ramifications for the thousands of people who have incorporated it into their daily lives, including myself.

But to be honest, none of that begins to compare to the profound experiences I have had or the discoveries I have made about my relationship to the creative process. I have had a chance to explore realms of experience that are unfamiliar to most people. My reason for writing this book is to share the insights I have gleaned from these experiences, with the intention that they will serve as guideposts for you in your own exploration of Deep Creativity.

This is NOT a how-to book. Deep Creativity is much more a matter of passion than of talent or training. If you throw yourself into anything with the single-mindedness and intensity demonstrated by the artists and mystics whose reflections you will read here, you will discover the same basic truths I have. These truths can be revolutionary in their impact on your life, your way of thinking, and your relationship to the world at large. But they are only accessible if you keep a completely open mind. Some of what you are about to discover may seem like science fiction or fantasy at first. I have confirmed every bit of it repeatedly through direct experience, and I invite you to do the same. Never take my word for it if you can experience it for yourself.

*Deep Creativity* is unlike anything else you are likely to encounter. It is built on Ten Tenets that form the foundation of Deep Creativity as a field of endeavor. These tenets represent a radical departure from the conventional wisdom of creativity research.

Most creativity books go over the same theories and research that have dominated the study of creativity for the past several decades. One of the ways to evaluate what you read about creativity is by asking yourself: *Does this feel new and fresh?* If you get the feeling that you have heard it all before, then the approach to creativity presented by the author is not particularly creative. I promise that what you are about to read will bear no resemblance to the ideas you will find in the ever-growing list of popular creativity books. Even more exciting, you are about to undergo a major transformation in terms of how you think about the world. After all, isn't that what a creativity book should do?

## CHAPTER 1

# Creativity without the Box

*"Creativity can be described as letting go of certainties."*
*—Gail Sheehy*

In Deep Creativity, the process matters far more than the product. Through this process, the artist comes in contact with an extraordinary source of joy, fulfillment, and transformation. If we draw the analogy between creativity and juice extraction, the artist is far more likely to see the process as the juice of the fruit, whereas scientists and the general public may look for the juice in whatever product remains at the end. For the artist, the finished work is more like the rind; all of the psychological and spiritual nourishment has been extracted through the creative experience. "The object isn't to make art," wrote Robert Henri in *The Art Spirit*, "it's to be in that wonderful state which makes art inevitable."[9]

Fortunately, some of the inspirational qualities of that experience remain in the product and get conveyed to the public. That is the function of great art. When we look up at the Sistine Chapel, listen to a Mozart sonata, or encounter a

Walt Whitman poem, we might just get an inkling of what the artist experienced during the creative process. In this regard, the value of the product cannot be dismissed. But our results-oriented society tends to place more emphasis on the product than the process, which allows people to overlook what is most essential and exciting about creativity. The scientific community is particularly susceptible to this oversight.

When we shift the priority from the product to the process, we can begin to see creativity in a new light. Old assumptions fall away, and we gain fresh insights into the nature of creativity, beginning with this:

## Tenet #1: Creativity is not what you think.

Two separate points can be found in this one statement. The first is that the tendency to equate creativity with thinking is misguided and unproductive. Albert Einstein once said, "The intellect has little to do on the road to discovery."[10] Considering the source, this assertion may come as a bit of a surprise. After all, Einstein's intellect is perceived as one of the most powerful and far-reaching in human history. And yet, when it comes to the creative process, he recognized that there were other forces at play—ones that extend beyond logic and rationality. To say the least, Einstein's position is a radical one; the psychologists who study creativity have not yet caught up to it.

For the most part, creativity researchers assume that new thoughts emerge simply by recombining existing ones. While there is no question that this can and does happen at times, the danger lies in reducing all creativity to mere computation. If all thoughts arise from other thoughts, then where did the first thought come from? Here is the logical flaw in this argument. In philosophy, it is known as an *infinite regress* problem, which means that the sequence of reasoning has no end. To say that old thoughts give rise to new ones does not explain creativity at all, because at some point in the past, a new thought had to be created without relying on the existence of another thought. In fact, existing thoughts may often serve as a barrier to the creative process.

We often hear the aphorism: "Think outside the box." The reason this advice makes no sense is that our thinking creates the box in the first place. If we want to understand creativity truly and deeply, we have to jettison the thought processes that handcuff our own creative capacities so that we can begin moving into the experiential realm where creativity resides. Rather than thinking outside the box, we must live outside it.

There is a second point to be found in Tenet #1. Creativity is not what you might think it is or expect it to be. If you have been influenced by the research literature, then some of your assumptions about creativity may be unsound. For instance, you may think that creativity is the domain only of certain exceptional or eminent individuals, whose creative gifts are linked to their superior intellect. But it turns out that the relationship between creativity and intelligence is not particularly strong. In fact, research with dementia patients has shown that the loss of brain function can actually enhance certain artistic abilities.[11] Even our most basic ideas about the nature of creativity can be called into question.

## Redefining Creativity

One of the biggest hurdles to overcome, if we seek a deeper understanding of creativity, has to do with the way it has been defined. The textbook definition of creativity identifies two criteria for something to be creative: *novelty* and *value*. Novelty means that the creative product must be outside the realm of what is acceptable, traditional or standard. In a testing situation, researchers look for responses that are statistically unusual, meaning that they occur rarely in a population. Value means that the creative product is useful or adaptive, addressing a particular need, serving some function or providing a certain degree of benefit to someone in our society. This criterion exists to help distinguish creativity from the ramblings of lunatics, who may generate novel streams of information that make no sense to anyone else and serve no apparent purpose.

Neither criterion aligns particularly well with the realities of the creative process. Artists engaged in this process are generally unconcerned with either novelty or value. When it comes to novelty, their experience is not lessened by knowing that someone else arrived at a certain idea or conclusion before they did. And value is something that others assign to their work. Artists already know that each creative experience is inherently valuable, regardless of the outcome.

When we focus on the process instead of the product, two very different criteria for creativity emerge: *freshness* and *transcendence*.

## Freshness

This is the felt sense that the particular experience you are having is unique and extraordinary. Although freshness and novelty may appear similar, they are as different as first-person and third-person approaches. Freshness is a subjective determination made by the artist based on the intensity of what is being experienced at this moment. We can mistake freshness for novelty because the first experience of a certain kind tends to have the greatest intensity for most people. With each repetition, spontaneity disappears, and the intensity diminishes as a result of habituation. But for the individual who is mindful, each experience feels fresh. You can do exactly the same thing every day, but if you love it with a passion and are fully present in the moment, you will feel as if you are doing it for the first time.

I had the privilege to live in Italy for three months, in a picturesque Umbrian hill town called Orvieto. In the center of the town sits a magnificent cathedral, the Duomo di Orvieto, which draws millions of tourists every year. The first time I saw the façade of the Duomo, with its golden mosaics, elaborate statuary, and huge bronze doors, I was so overwhelmed by its beauty that I could hardly speak. I continued to visit the Duomo on a nearly daily basis for the duration of my stay; each time it had a similar effect on me. The experience of looking at that façade never lost its freshness—not once. The artists that created this magnificent work managed to capture and convey some element of their own inspiration that continues to be felt by admirers like myself more than six centuries later.

When you encounter the reflections of great artists, you get the sense of their overwhelming capacity for freshness. Composer Peter Tchaikovsky told an interviewer, "It would be vain to try to put into words the immeasurable sense of bliss which comes over me directly when a new idea awakens in me and begins to assume a definite form. I forget everything and behave like a madman: everything within me starts pulsing and quivering."[12]

Although Tchaikovsky mentions the awakening of new ideas, the intensity he describes is not dependent on novelty. A case in point is the occurrence of unintentional plagiarism, which is particularly common among songwriters and composers. One day you wake up with a melody in your head, which you are thrilled to discover. Later, you find out that the melody was one you had heard before, perhaps on the radio. The fact that someone else had already composed it does not take away from the freshness of your creative experience.

## Transcendence

This second defining quality of creativity has to do with the experience of moving beyond your own limitations. As you engage in the creative process, you may get a sense of expanding your knowledge base, breaking through false or restrictive assumptions, uncovering new thought processes, restructuring your worldview, solving a mystery, or discovering new abilities. The creative process tends to stretch you in some way, pushing you in terms of your ability to respond to circumstances that are far beyond the ordinary.

Within those extraordinary circumstances lies the passageway to a fundamental and profoundly fulfilling realm of experience—one that is likely to be inaccessible to most people in most situations. Mary Wigman, the expressionist dance pioneer, described it this way: "During the process of artistic creation, man descends into the primordial elements of life. He reverts to himself to become lost in something greater than himself, in the immediate, indivisible essence of life."[13]

Here, Wigman captures two very important ideas related to Deep Creativity. One is that the creative process leads to an essential, core layer of reality. Two is that this reality can only be accessed by losing yourself. The most important form of transcendence, in terms of Deep Creativity, is self-transcendence. In the creative process, the artist escapes the restrictions of personal identity in order to become something altogether different, as we are about to see.

# CHAPTER 2

# Transcendent Imagination

*"Imagination rules the world."*
*—Napoleon Bonaparte*

The creative process takes many forms, which can vary from one individual to the next. In some well-known cases, artists have maintained that their creative style is mechanistic. For instance, pointillist painter Georges Seurat eschewed the idea of creative inspiration, relying instead on new technologies and theories of form and expression as his primary influences. Commenting on the public's response to his work, he asserted, "They see poetry in what I have done. No. I apply my methods and that is all there is to it."[14]

## Self-Transcendence

Regardless of the accuracy of Seurat's claims pertaining to his own work, there is no denying that creative inspiration has played a key role in the creation of much of the world's most beloved art, literature, and innovation. And inspiration is inherently a transformative process. Many artists claim to undergo a personal transformation through the creative process, ending up at a very different point than where they started. This leads us to a second fundamental principle of Deep Creativity:

## Tenet #2: All creating is becoming.

Novelists, playwrights, and actors often describe the experience of embodying the characters they are creating. Similarly, artists may feel a sense of merging with their subject. D.H. Lawrence captured the essence of this experience when he observed, "Art is a form of supremely delicate awareness and atonement—meaning at oneness, the state of being at one with the object."[15]

Musicians and composers have reported the sensation of channeling what John Lennon called "the music that surpasses understanding."[16] Composer Richard Wagner felt that he could merge into a universal current of sound vibration: "I feel that I am one with this vibrating force, that it is omniscient, and that I can draw upon it to an extent that is limited only by my capacity to do so."[17]

Electronic recording artist Steve Roach merges into the sound stream he is creating by immersing himself completely in his compositions. As he is working on a new piece, he runs it through a sound system that fills every room of his house. That way, the sound penetrates his awareness continuously throughout his day—even while he sleeps. And he may work on a single composition for weeks or months at a time.

Scientists are more reluctant to acknowledge their experience of merging with their subject matter, perhaps because of their concern for objectivity. But as quantum physicists have shown, this concern may be based on a misconception about scientific objectivity. "The world is given to me only once, not one existing and one perceived," wrote physicist Erwin Schrodinger. "Subject and object are only one. The barrier between them cannot be said to have broken down as a result of recent experience in the physical sciences, for this barrier does not exist."[18]

Entomologist Bob Sluss once confided to me that his understanding of insects stemmed from his ability to experience the world from their perspective.

"I have moments when I can feel what it's like to be a wasp," he told me. "That's how I learn most effectively about their behavior."[19]

To become something or someone different than yourself requires that you move beyond the boundaries of your own identity. This is self-transcendence, and it is also the starting point of Deep Creativity. In describing their creative experiences, artists often talk about the sensation of disappearing or losing oneself. For instance, abstract expressionist painter Betty Parsons said, "The best things happen in the great painters when the artist gets lost and something else takes over."[20]

This loss of personal identity does not happen by accident. In many cases, the individual seeks it out. Andrew Wyeth observed, "When I paint, I try to obliterate Andy Wyeth."[21] At its core, the experience of self-transcendence is infinitely gratifying and joyous. Recent research has shown that the capacity to have such experiences not only predicts our overall well-being but actually gives rise to it.

Late in his life, psychologist Abraham Maslow came to the conclusion that self-transcendence is the ultimate human drive.[22] In the 1940's, Maslow first proposed his *hierarchy of needs*, a brilliant model that ties together all of the major theories of motivation that had been put forth by personality psychologists. Anyone who has taken an introductory psychology course has seen this pyramid depicting the various levels of motivation in Maslow's hierarchy:

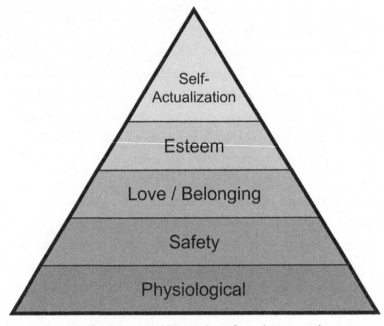

Maslow's original hierarchy-of-needs pyramid

According to Maslow, the most basic needs—those at the bottom of the pyramid—must be met before the individual can begin to address the "higher" ones. Originally, Maslow placed *self-actualization* at the top of his pyramid. This is the universal need to come into our own by realizing our personal potential and becoming most fully ourselves.

Three years before his death, Maslow reconceived his hierarchy, adding an extra layer to the top of his pyramid:

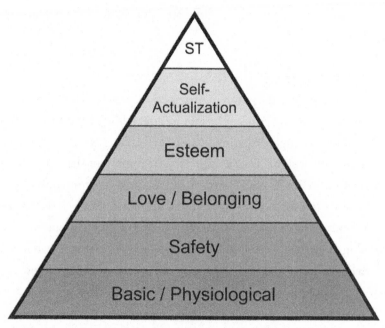

Maslow's modified hierarchy-of-needs pyramid, which includes self-transcendence at the top

This final formulation of Maslow's model treats self-transcendence as the highest level of human development. Those who arrive at the top of the hierarchy seek and find gratification through communion with something beyond themselves, such as a cause, ideal, or higher power.

The drive for self-transcendence is not age-dependent. Some individuals discover it early in life. In his memoirs, Russian abstract painter Wassily Kandinsky wrote, "Even as a child, drawing allowed me to live outside time and space so that I was no longer aware of myself."[23] For others, self-transcendence may never become a particularly compelling need. It is possible to reach the end of one's life without ever having experienced it or even being aware of what one has missed.

Yet Deep Creativity depends on this drive. Without self-transcendence, we cannot undergo the necessary shift in perspective that gives rise to new insights and new possibilities. Only when we are freed of the constraints of our own identity can we become something different. The key to this transformation is imagination.

## Imagination and Empathy

Never underestimate the power of imagination, which can take you anywhere in the universe. At age 16, Albert Einstein imagined himself riding on a beam of light. That simple thought experiment inspired his later work on relativity and led him to the conclusion, "Imagination is more important than knowledge."[24]

Imagination makes it possible for a Mozart to hear symphonies that have not yet been written or a Tesla to envision the workings of devices that have never been built. What an extraordinary power this is! Through our imagination, we can adopt any vantage point. For at least a brief moment, we can know what it feels like to be a bird soaring and gliding up above, the wind blowing through a stand of trees, a sea creature at the bottom of the ocean, a nebula turning into a star system, a quark moving deep inside an atom, or—perhaps most intriguingly—another human being.

If we allow ourselves, we can see through the eyes of another and feel what is in their heart. This is empathy, but it is also an act of imagination. First, we make the intention to share in another person's experience. Then, we imagine that experience and eventually we feel it as our own. Essentially, we create ourselves in another's image. Empathy is pertinent to Deep Creativity because it follows the basic principle of creating by becoming. When we transform ourselves into someone else—taking on their joy as well as their suffering—we can gain the kinds of extraordinary insights that are at the core of great art, literature, science, poetry, and technology.

What makes a painting, a piece of music, or an invention so compelling is that it captures a profound experience of our common humanity. I am drawn to the product of someone else's creativity because it speaks to my own experience in some way. The artist has managed to establish an empathic bond with me, sometimes reaching out to touch my heart across centuries or millennia. I see something of myself in Michelangelo's David, am filled with tenderness as I gaze at the Taj Mahal, and am elevated to the heavens when listening to liturgical music composed by Hildegard of Bingen over eight centuries ago. How is this possible?

The creative process allows the artist to tap into something that transcends individual identity and that binds one human being to another. Let's look at the mysterious nature of that transcendent "something."

# CHAPTER 3

# The Mysterious Source

*"Art evokes the mystery without which the world would not exist."*
*—Rene Magritte*

Throughout history, artists and thinkers have attributed their creativity to a mysterious source existing well beyond the scope of their own conscious minds. "The work comes into the world at an undetermined hour, from a source still unknown, but it comes inevitably," claimed Wassily Kandinsky.[25] Regarding the mysterious nature of creativity, Albert Einstein observed, "There comes a leap in consciousness, call it intuition or what you will, and the solutions come to you, and you don't know how or why."[26]

This tendency to describe a creative source outside of oneself does not appear to be simply a matter of humility, either genuine or false. In his biography of the Beatles, Mark Hertsgaard wrote, "Lennon once said that he and McCartney were both egomaniacs, yet he could speak quite humbly about this aspect of songwriting. It wasn't any particular genius that made Paul and him great composers, he maintained; they were merely vehicles that 'the music of the spheres, the music that surpasses understanding' passed through on its way into the world."[27]

The modern psychological explanation for this type of experience is that creativity arises from *the unconscious*. But is this really an explanation? The use of this term, "the unconscious," lends itself to inexactitude. Over a century ago, William James recognized this problem in his classic work, *The Principles of Psychology*. "The distinction between the unconscious and the conscious," James observed, "is the sovereign means for believing what one likes in psychology, and of turning what might become a science into a tumbling-ground for whimsies."[28]

James did not have an issue with the idea that some of our mental activity, including creativity, may take place unconsciously. His concern had more to do with this thing called "the unconscious." What is it? A part of the brain? If so, where is it to be found? Why does the unconscious seem to be able to do things that the conscious mind cannot? Is the unconscious smarter than we are? If so, how is this possible? Postulating this mysterious entity called "the unconscious" does not answer fundamental questions about the inner workings or ultimate source of creativity. Instead, it passes the buck, from an intellectual standpoint, providing a box where the creative mystery can be stored, rather than any real insight into the nature of that mystery.

Creative individuals have often provided a very different answer to the question: *What is the source of your creativity?* In one of his poems, Henry Wadsworth Longfellow wrote, "Art is the gift of God."[29] Johann Brahms told one biographer, "Straightaway the ideas flow in upon me, directly from God."[30] Describing the inspiration for one of his most acclaimed operas, *Madame Butterfly*, Puccini noted, "The music of this opera was dictated to me by God; I was merely instrumental in putting it on paper and communicating it to the public."[31]

Now, I am not claiming to reject the unconscious as a source of creativity in favor of a higher power. Actually, my claim is that both explanations are grasping at the exact same thing; they only differ in terms of the label they assign to it. Whether you call it "the unconscious" or "God," the source is the same. This leads us to one of the boldest and most important ideas in Deep Creativity, which is a precursor to our third tenet: *All creativity emanates from a single source.*

There is a tendency to think that ideas and insights arise from the independent genius of the individual, but this assumption has never aligned with the experiences described by artists that have lived and created in every era and every part of the world. It limits our understanding of the process and does not qualify as a valid scientific theory, for reasons that I will soon explain.

Instead, I want you to consider a bold alternative, which is that *every human creation throughout history can be attributed to a single source.* Whether we consider Mozart's symphonies, Edison's inventions, Frida Kahlo's paintings, Ernest Hemingway's novels, or Maya Angelou's poetry, the ultimate source is the same. There has only ever been one creator—a single consciousness inhabiting myriad forms.

I know this to be true through direct experience. In other words, my way of arriving at this discovery has been completely empirical. Although science is built on empiricism, which is the notion that all knowledge comes from experience, the scientific community often rejects certain types of experiences that it considers to be "non-ordinary." Whereas artists depend on revelation as a source of creative inspiration, scientists argue that this type of experience cannot be reproduced. The revelation I am about to describe is one that I have had on numerous occasions, which makes it reproducible, as far as I am concerned. And by the time you finish this book, my intention is that this type of experience will be just as reproducible for you. In no way do I expect you to accept any idea you find here, based simply on my authority. I urge you to find out for yourself.

In December 2014, I had a vision that changed my life. Suddenly, I had a clear memory of a point beyond time or space. The sensation was unmistakable. I remembered what it was like to be expansive and limitless; to not be confined to a physical body; and to exist simultaneously at every level of creation, from galaxies to subatomic particles. At that moment, I knew at my core that there is and has only ever been one consciousness. This consciousness may inhabit many forms and take on a multitude of experiences, but it is always the same. Every possible experience that can be known or felt has a single "experiencer," if you will.

When I was first exposed to the *Book of Genesis* as a child, I remember wondering about the bold statement: "In the beginning, God created heaven and earth." How does one create a universe? With the power of my imagination, I tried to envision a supreme being building something out of nothing. But given that the starting point was "formless and void," I could not wrap my head around it. The mystery of creation always remained exactly that to me.

Then, in my moment of revelation, I had the answer: There is one unified consciousness from which all creation arises—including human creativity. Two weeks after my initial revelation, I heard these words while looking at a familiar image: *The source is entangled in the universe.* In other words, the creation is an embodiment of the creator. If you go looking for the source of all creation, do not search beyond yourself and your own surroundings. Everything you can see, hear, smell, taste, and touch is a manifestation of the one consciousness from which it arises.

The idea that all form emanates from a single source holds great power. For one thing, it offers creativity researchers something that all scientists seek, which is *parsimony*. In science, the simpler explanation is always preferable. Why introduce many factors to explain something when one will do? This is really an aesthetic issue; the simpler explanation just feels better—cleaner and more elegant. At the same time, there are functional advantages to simplicity. It seems that simpler theories give rise to new discoveries and ways of thinking.

In terms of understanding creativity, a theory that attributes all ideas to one source accounts for the fact that many minds can converge on the same discoveries simultaneously, as in the case of Charles Darwin and Alfred Wallace. Both published their theories of natural selection in the same year. We have many other examples of this throughout history, such as the formulation of calculus by Newton and Liebniz, the discovery of oxygen by Priestley and Lavoisier, or the race to find the structure of DNA. Scientists have terms to describe this phenomenon, such as *multiple discovery* or *simultaneous invention*. But what they have lacked is an adequate explanation—until now.

Our single-source model also accounts for the *phenomenology* of creativity, which is contained in the first-person accounts of creative individuals concerning their personal experiences. Often, these individuals report the felt sense of their greatest ideas and breakthroughs coming from an unknown source—one that extends far beyond the limits of their own minds.

The Beatles are a perfect example of this. John Lennon and Paul McCartney often observed that the source of their songs was something of a mystery to them. In describing his creative process, John Lennon once noted:

> My joy is when you're like possessed, like a medium, you know. I'll be sitting around and it'll come in the middle of the night or at the time when you don't want to do it—that's the exciting part. So, I'm lying around and then this thing comes as a whole piece, you know, words and music, and I think well, you know, can I say I wrote it? I don't know who the hell wrote it—I'm just sitting here and this whole damned song comes out.[32]

Similarly, McCartney claims that the melody to the song "Yesterday" came to him one morning while awakening from sleep. The writing process in that case felt more like transcribing something that had been given to him, as opposed to working on a composition. He likened the experience to "pulling it out of the air."[33]

Artists often report the sense of being a channel for something that is not their own. George Eliot, the Victorian female writer who adopted a male pseudonym, claimed that something "not herself" took possession of her, and that she felt her own personality to be "merely the instrument through which this spirit, as it were, was acting."[34]

This metaphor of the artist as musical instrument is a common theme. A second female George, French novelist George Sand, wrote, "The Wind plays my old harp as it lists. It is the other who sings as he likes, well or ill, and when I try to think about it, I am afraid and tell myself that I am nothing, nothing at all."[35] In a similar vein, sculptor August Rodin observed, "Artists and thinkers are like lyres, infinitely delicate and sonorous, whose vibrations, awakened by the circumstances of each epoch, are prolonged to the ears of all other mortals."[36]

Our single-source model offers simplicity. Rather than trying to understand creativity from the individual perspective of every artist that ever lived, we can go directly to the source. Creativity becomes a more manageable phenomenon to study and grasp if it is seen as arising from one source as opposed to billions. At the same time, this model also raises any number of questions: How does one source yield multiple perspectives? If every human being can tap into the same source, why don't we all have equal creative ability? Why is it that some minds appear to be far more creative than others? And what can be done to enhance our connection to the source of our creativity? Tackling these questions is the challenge that lies ahead.

# CHAPTER 4

# Consciousness in Mind

*"Bottomless wonders spring from simple rules,*
*which are repeated without end."*
—*Benoit Mandelbrot*

I f I am going to make the bold assertion that all creativity comes from a single source, I need to explain how this source interacts uniquely with the mind of each individual artist. To do this, I will need to draw a distinction between *consciousness* and *mind*.

As brilliant as modern psychologists and neuroscientists may be, I have always been mystified by one blind spot that most of them share: the tendency to confound these two concepts. The blind spot may date back to the father of American psychology, William James, who identified the five defining characteristics of consciousness in his 1890 *Principles of Psychology*. The problem is that these characteristics pertain to mind—not consciousness. James got it wrong, and the researchers that have followed in his footsteps have perpetuated this mistake.

The distinction between consciousness and mind (see Appendix 2) can be summed up in this analogy, drawn from Buddhist psychology: consciousness is the sky and the mind is the set of clouds moving across it. The mind encompasses everything we know through the faculties of sensation, attention, perception, memory, language, learning, reasoning, problem-solving, and decision-making. Consciousness, on the other hand, encompasses everything we are. Descartes offered the famous phrase, *I think, therefore I am.* Here is my amended—and perhaps a little twisted—version of it: *I am, therefore I am conscious.*

Descartes was attempting to construct a statement that was true beyond any doubt. The fact that one can think, and therefore doubt one's own existence, is the very proof of that existence. My concern is completely different. I am interested in the relationship between consciousness and creativity.

## Infinite and Mysterious

So far, we have established that all creativity emanates from a single source, and that this source creates by becoming. Assuming that we ourselves have been created by this source, then it follows that this source is embedded in each of us. When we say "I am," we are acknowledging the source that created us and that also permeates our being. This source is pure consciousness. Now you can begin to see the significance of the statement: *I am, therefore I am conscious.* Given that I exist, I must emanate from the source of all creation, which is consciousness itself, and therefore I must be imbued with it.

Now, we have arrived at one of the most profound principles of Deep Creativity:

*Tenet #3: Consciousness is the ultimate source of all creation, including human creativity.*

Consciousness is essence. Our essence can be defined as our fundamental or intrinsic nature. The word comes from the Latin *esse,* meaning "to be." Simply by existing, we are imbued with the pure consciousness that is the essence and origin of all things, including our own creativity. To learn more about the nature of this source, we turn to the real experts: the mystics of the world. Considered among India's great mystical texts, the Hindu *Upanishads* state:

> In the beginning was only Being,
> One without a second.
> Out of himself he brought forth the cosmos
> And entered into everything in it.
> There is nothing that does not come from him.
> Of everything he is the inmost Self.[37]

Here, "Being" refers to consciousness, which in its purest form can be considered an indivisible unity. The unity of consciousness transcends everything, including all thought and all distinctions. There is no room for separation: No self or other. No life or death. No light or dark. No known or unknown. And in the words of an even more ancient Hindu text, the *Rig Veda*, there is "neither existence nor non-existence."[38] This is why consciousness is also void. If everything is unified in the realm of consciousness, then absolutely nothing exists there as a separate entity.

Consciousness has no limits, although the thoughts and images that arise from it are highly limited. Thoughts limit our experience and our universe by drawing distinctions such as: male and female, good and evil, black and white. These are the mental clouds moving across the sky of consciousness. The sky itself is expansive and exists beyond any and all distinctions.

Remember the infinite regress problem? Our limited thoughts cannot simply arise from other thoughts. At some point in the distant past, at least one thought must have emerged from some other source. Here's why: We cannot generate one finite thing from another infinitely. There has to be an infinite source of everything finite. According to Buddhist scripture, "There is an unborn, unmade, unbecome and incomposite; for if there were not, there would be no escape from what is born, made, become, or compounded."[39]

Scientists and Zen masters alike have expressed this idea that human creativity comes from an infinite source. Physicist David Bohm refers to this source as "the immeasurable" and explains why anything that can be measured or defined, including all of human thought, has to emerge from it. "Original and creative insight within the whole field of measure is the action of the immeasurable," writes Bohm in *Wholeness and the Implicate Order*. "For when such insight occurs, the source cannot be within ideas already contained in the field of measure but rather in the immeasurable, which contains the essential formative cause of all that happens in the field of measure."[40]

Sogyal Rinpoche refers to the source of creativity as "mysterious" because of the fact that it exists beyond the scope of thought: "Each individual act and manifestation of creativity, whether it is in music, art, or poetry, or indeed in the moments and unfoldings of scientific discovery, as many scientists have described, arises from a mysterious ground of inspiration and is mediated into form by a translating and communicating energy."[41]

Zen master D. T. Suzuki observes that the process described in creation myths "is not historical, not accidental, not at all measurable. It goes on continuously without cessation, with no beginning, with no end. It is not an event of yesterday or today or tomorrow, it comes out of timelessness, of nothingness, of Absolute Void...in an absolute present."[42]

Artists often refer to consciousness as something unknown or mysterious. William Zorach, the traditionalist sculptor and author of *Art is My Life*, viewed his own creative process as a "journey into the unknown regions."[43] French poet and adventurer Arthur Rimbaud used similar language: "I want to be a poet, and I am working to make myself a visionary...to arrive at *the unknown*...through a long, a prodigious and rational disordering of all my senses."[44] For D. H. Lawrence, the creative process that gave rise to his poetry and prose involved "touching the unknown, the real unknown, the unknown unknown."[45]

Albert Einstein saw consciousness as an impenetrable mystery and insisted that it was the source of his greatest ideas and discoveries:

> The fairest thing we can experience is the mysterious. It was the experience of mystery—even if mixed with fear—that engendered religion. A knowledge of the existence of something we cannot penetrate, of the manifestations of the profoundest reason and the most radiant beauty, which are only accessible to

our reason in their most elementary forms—it is this knowledge and this emotion that constitute the truly religious attitude; in this sense, and in this sense alone, I am a deeply religious man.[46]

Why would consciousness be described as a mystery? The answer is quite simple. The essential nature of consciousness cannot be penetrated by human thought. No matter how we try, we can never know it conceptually because it extends beyond any representational system. All attempts to grasp it are destined to fail.

## Universal Mind

Consciousness exists within each of us as pure being, pure experience with no limits. In trying to comprehend it, the best we can do is draw pictures and analogies. I find it helpful to think of it as the eternal dance between perfect unity, where all things merge into one, and perfect void, where nothing exists at all. If we picture unity as light and void as darkness, then consciousness might be depicted as follows:

Consciousness depicted as an alternating pattern of light and dark.

In this image, the blackness of void encompasses the whiteness of unity, and vice versa, illustrating that unity and void are inseparable. The image itself is only a point of reference. After all, we are trying to depict something that cannot be depicted because it has no limits. What matters most, as we grapple with the fundamentals of Deep Creativity, is the idea that essence and non-essence are inextricably linked within consciousness.

So, how does consciousness generate the vast array of thoughts contained within the minds of all human beings? As you can imagine, this question has a complex answer. The unity of consciousness has to be shattered in such a way as to give rise to multiplicity. How this happens is the topic of the next chapter. In the meantime, let us assume that such a shattering has taken place. Now what?

In an instant, consciousness is transformed into the *universal mind*. The eternal dance of essence and non-essence is replicated millions of times over, in the form of individual thoughts. What is a thought, after all? Thoughts are patterns of light and dark, essence and non-essence, 1's and 0's. There is a reason that computers use binary code. All knowledge—including letters, numbers, images and sounds—can be represented and stored as patterns consisting of only two types of information. Consider a simple concept such as *cat*. Contained in this concept is information about what a cat is (four-legged, furry, feline), but also about what a cat is <u>not</u> (dog, human, bird, snake). Every thought includes the same dance of essence and non-essence found within the pure consciousness from which it emerges.

Just as there is only one consciousness, there is also only one universal mind. It holds all of the patterns and permutations that arise from the dance of essence and non-essence. Every single thought that has ever been generated can be found in this universal mind

## The Mandelbrot Set

In the last chapter, I mentioned that I was looking at a familiar image when I heard the following words: *The source is entangled in the universe*. That image was of the *Mandelbrot set*, which I consider to be one of the most important discoveries in human history. For me, the Mandelbrot set represents, among other things, a map of the universal mind. The reason for this association will soon become clear.

I had first encountered images of the Mandelbrot set in 1994. A mathematician friend displayed them as part of a slide show to a group of party guests. For some reason, audiences laugh when I recount this story. I guess it seems strange to imagine a group of partygoers looking at solutions to mathematical equations. But I would say that this party was a life-changing experience for me. So, it turns out that showing images of the Mandelbrot set—no matter how strange that may seem—is not a particularly bad way to entertain your party guests!

At the time, I had no idea that this is what I was seeing. All I knew is that the images were extremely powerful and compelling. Here are a few of the images I saw that night:

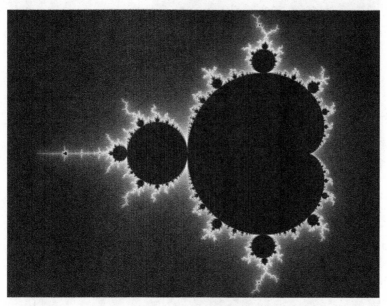

Classic depiction of the Mandelbrot

Zooming into the previous image

An even deeper zoom

Only much later did I begin to learn about the nature of *fractals*. A fractal is a never-ending pattern that is self-embedded, meaning that the same motif reappears at every level. Although there are many types of fractals, the Mandelbrot set is undoubtedly the most familiar and recognizable. It is the graphical representation of the solutions to an infinite set of mathematical equations. Essentially, the graph is generated by repeating a mathematical process over and over in an infinite loop.

For two decades, I did not give any thought to the set of images I had seen at that party. Then suddenly, I started seeing the Mandelbrot set when I closed my eyes. This went on for several days. I began looking for images—especially moving ones—that would give me some understanding of why I was being so drawn to this fractal. While watching an online video in which the camera zooms in on the Mandelbrot set, it suddenly struck me: *The Mandelbrot set depicts the universal mind!*

When consciousness, which is the source of creation, shatters into the vast array of thoughts that comprise the universal mind, something formless and limitless takes form and becomes limited. All the thoughts encompassed in the mind have their limits; in fact, their function is to impose limits. Although each thought is limited, it carries within it the same interplay of essence and non-essence that characterizes consciousness in its purest form.

The universal mind acts as an intermediary between consciousness and each individual mind. Here we make an important distinction between the universal mind, on the one hand, and the mind of the individual, on the other. What we call the universal mind is the vehicle through which consciousness becomes embedded at every level of the universe. This mind has the qualities of a fractal. Within any fractal, the same pattern repeats endlessly, no matter how big or small the scale. Mathematicians describe fractals as being "self-similar"; I prefer to think of them as self-embedded. The patterns occurring at different levels of a fractal are not just similar; they are identical. The same pattern embeds itself within itself infinitely.

Mind on a universal scale is a fractal, with consciousness serving as the recurring theme. Consciousness abides at every level of the universe. If you could zoom in on yourself, you would find consciousness in your entire body but also, as you looked more closely, in the organ systems, organs, tissue, cells, organelles, molecules, atoms, and subatomic particles that comprise your body.

If you zoomed out to the far reaches of the universe, you would discover the same thing. The universal mind is self-embedded.

The mental contents at each layer will certainly differ, just as they do from one individual to the next. But consciousness itself—the interplay of essence and non-essence—can be found everywhere. So, am I suggesting that inanimate objects, such as rocks or water, are conscious? Absolutely! From a modern scientific perspective, this may seem like a point of contention, but the world's great mystics have always known it:

> The first peace, which is the most important, is that which comes within the souls of men when they realize their relationship, their oneness, with the universe and all its powers, and when they realize that at the center of the universe dwells Wakan-Tanka, and that this center is really everywhere, it is within us.
>
> —Black Elk, Oglala Lakota shaman[47]

> Master Tung-kuo asked Chuang Tzu, "This thing called the Way—where does it exist?"
>
> Chuang Tzu said, "There's no place it doesn't exist."
>
> "Come," said Master Tung-kuo, "you must be more specific!"
>
> "It is in the ant."
>
> "As low a thing as that?"
>
> "It is in the panic grass."
>
> "But that's lower still!"
>
> "It is in the tiles and shards."
>
> "How can it be so low?"
>
> "It is in the piss and dung."
>
> —Chuang Tzu, Taoist master[48]

> The Divine Mother revealed to me in the Kali temple that it was She who had become everything. She showed me

that everything was full of Consciousness. The Image was Consciousness, the altar was Consciousness, the water-vessels were Consciousness, the door-sill was Consciousness, the marble floor was Consciousness—all was Consciousness.

    —Ramakrishna, Indian mystic and yogi[49]

To God belong the East and the West;
And wherever you turn,
there is the face of God.

    —*Qur'an*, Islamic holy text[50]

I am the Light that is above them all.
I am the All; the All came forth from Me
and the All attained to Me.
Cleave a piece of wood, I am there;
Lift up the stone and you will find Me there.

    —Jesus Christ in the *Gospel of Thomas*[51]

God is unified oneness—one without two, inestimable. Genuine divine existence engenders the existence of all of creation. The sublime, inner essences secretly constitute a chain linking everything from the highest to the lowest, extending from the upper pool to the edge of the universe.

    —Moses de Leon, *The Book of the Pomegranates*[52]

The universal mind distributes consciousness to even the most remote or unlikely places. When I began to envision the Mandelbrot set in my mind's eye, this is the entirety of the message I received: *The source is entangled in the universe, layer upon embedded layer. There are no boondocks.* So far, I have only shared the first part with you. Now, I can put the entire statement in perspective. Thinking of the universal mind as a fractal encompassing the entire universe, we begin to understand that the pure consciousness from which this mind arises is embedded at each layer of the fractal. But also, within a given layer, every coordinate represents an entry point into infinite layers where consciousness can be found.

Sometimes, we may think that we have been shortchanged by the universe. We may compare ourselves unfavorably to individuals who seem smarter, more attractive, or wealthier than us, and especially to those who appear more creative. If I mention my interest in creativity to someone, the person with whom I am conversing will often confess: "I'm not very creative." For years, I have wondered what would possess someone to make such an admission. The same person would be far less likely to confess that he or she is below average in intelligence, driving ability, or most other competencies—except perhaps mathematical ability.

Social psychologists have shown that there is a *self-serving bias* in our assessment of our own abilities, meaning that most of us tend to look favorably upon ourselves in general. We are likely to take full credit for our successes while attributing our failures to factors outside our control (such as bad luck). Self-serving bias occurs most commonly when comparing ourselves to others on dimensions that are either socially desirable or subjective. So, the tendency to rate ourselves as uncreative suggests one of two possibilities: a) creativity is not a particularly desirable quality; or b) we cannot hide from the fact that some people out there are far more creative than we are.

Given that creativity books, workshops and corporate training events generate hundreds of millions of dollars in revenue annually, I am going to dismiss the first possibility. Sure, some of the people we call "creative" seem highly susceptible to mental health issues such as depression or addiction. In some cases, they may be just plain weird. But there is no denying that we value what they are able to do. We might even wish that we could innovate like Steve Jobs or be as prolific as Joni Mitchell.

When we compare ourselves to great artists, we might simply fall short. There is no fooling ourselves about our creativity when we see how few masterpieces we have to our names. Chances are that nobody is admiring our paintings, using our inventions, or humming along to our melodies. Creativity measured as either the quantity or perceived quality of your creative output can be a particularly harsh standard by which to assess yourself. If you would rather relax with friends or watch a video than engage in creative pursuits, your artistic achievement might seem limited compared to someone who is continuously immersed in the creative process.

As you already know, artistic achievement is not the primary concern of Deep Creativity. Our attention is focused much more on the creative process than the product. In terms of that process, each of us has equal access to the source of all creativity. That is why there are "no boondocks." None of us has ever been shortchanged when it comes to our location within this fractal called the universal mind. We are all connected to consciousness, which is embedded infinitely within that mind.

Just because a limitless source of knowledge and creativity is available to you in theory does not necessarily mean that you will be able to access it. Each individual mind represents a tiny subset of the universal mind. Of all the possible thoughts available to us, we can only access a relatively miniscule portion. Our minds' limitations are self-imposed, although these limitations are undoubtedly shaped by both genetic and environmental factors.

Try to think about your own mind. What does it do well? The most impressive thing about the individual mind is its ability to detect patterns. Each of us is born with no knowledge of language. Yet, by the age of six, we have an expressive vocabulary (what we can use in speech) of 2500 words and a receptive vocabulary (what we can understand) of more than 20,000! This is a remarkable feat, especially considering that we are also able to master many of the grammatical rules and subtleties of our native language in this relatively short amount of time.

The extraordinary human capacity to find and recognize patterns can account for every mental ability, including memory, logic, perception, and concept-formation. Of all the concepts we use on a daily basis, perhaps the most intriguing is our self-concept. In one sense, the self-concept is just another thought. Like any other thought, it is simply a pattern of light and dark, essence and non-essence, 1's and 0's. Through the self-concept, our minds define and therefore limit what we are and what we know. With respect to the self, we establish a pattern that determines the entire sum of our knowledge concerning the world around us and our relationship to it.

In other words, each of our minds is a self-imposed pattern. Of all the possible thoughts available to us, we shine the light of our attention on only a small subset, leaving the vast majority of thoughts in the darkness. Where we shine our individual light is determined by how we define ourselves and our capabilities. Each person's mind enforces the limits of what it can know. We decide which patterns are worthy of our attention, but also how worthy our attention is of those patterns. If we tell ourselves that something is outside of our grasp, it certainly will be. Overcoming this self-imposed restriction is the key to the creative process.

CHAPTER 5

# The Creation Cycle

*"What was scattered gathers. What was gathered blows away."*
*—Heraclitus*

Most of the time, we are locked into a specific perspective on the world. The self-concept we adopt determines how we shine the light of our attention, which in turn shapes what we know and understand. In the shadows, far outside our range of awareness, lies the perspective of "the other." Of all the mysteries we face as human beings, perhaps nothing is more mysterious than the contents of someone else's mind, including their knowledge, thoughts, and experiences.

One of the basic tenets of Deep Creativity is that all creating is becoming. But to become someone or something other than ourselves, we must find a way to delve into what might seem like an impenetrable mystery. With respect to that mystery, there are essentially three types of creative experiences, which either: a) hide the mystery; b) illuminate the mystery; or c) transcend the mystery.

Most of what we do, as human beings, is reinforce the boundaries of the self. Just consider the mainstream media. Every day, enormous amounts of informational content are being created and disseminated. Most of the programming we encounter is designed to keep us focused on ourselves. In the news, we learn about events that impact our lives in some way—weather, traffic, politics, and sports. We are entertained by shows and movies that deal with situations to which we can relate personally. Programming intended to distract us from our own problems and concerns often does so at someone else's expense. We might feel better about ourselves by learning about the failings and foibles of others, ranging from the rich and famous to the poor and unsung.

This type of content requires a certain amount of creativity to generate, but it serves only to conceal the mystery of what is to be found in the hearts and minds of others. Great art, on the other hand, illuminates that mystery by giving us a glimpse into the perspectives and emotions of others. Picasso's *Guernica,* for example, conveys the chaos and suffering of war. The *Pietà* by Michelangelo takes us inside a mother's grief. When listening to an inspired piece of music or reciting a poem, we may be transported beyond the limitations of our own minds and given a sense of connection to something greater—an ideal, a sensation, or a different time or place.

On rare occasions, the creative process goes even farther. The distinction between self and other gets blurred completely. We gain clarity into our true nature, which is the nature of all things. If the source of all creation is consciousness, then it follows that the source abides equally in everybody and everything. Liberated from the distinctions imposed by our minds, we gain access into the realm of consciousness, where such distinctions have no dominion. The mystery of "the other" exists only within a mind that distinguishes the other from itself. Beyond the limits of the mind, such distinctions are meaningless.

When the creative process manages to transcend the mystery of the other, the end result can be profound. Just consider the teachings of Jesus or Buddha. Jesus said, "Love your enemies and pray for those who persecute you."[53] This imperative poses a great challenge to the individual mind, forcing it to transcend the distinction not just between *self* and *other*, but also between *friend* and *enemy*. When we look past the actions of individuals to see their true essence, these distinctions just fall away. We are able to realize that our interconnecting consciousness takes precedence over any thoughts or actions stemming from the limited perspective of our individual minds.

The Buddha offered a specific way to end suffering—a method grounded in the Four Noble Truths. The second of these Truths is that suffering arises from ignorance concerning the nature of reality in general and the self in particular. According to the Buddha, there is no separate, autonomous self. If we are able to see through the delusion of this small, individual self, we can experience something that transcends birth and death, not to mention the distinctions separating us from others.

Both of those great teachers, Jesus and Buddha, undertook a journey inward that allowed them to transcend the mystery of the other. Each of them created a pathway for those of us who aspire to follow in their footsteps. Their path is not a straight line but rather a circle. Through a cyclical process called the *creation cycle*, consciousness embeds itself in the very limited thought forms of the human mind and then returns inevitably to its original, unlimited form.

## Beyond Linear Thinking

Like everything else in nature, the creative process has to be cyclical. The field of ecology has established that the atoms and molecules found in nature cycle through different stages. For instance, the oxygen cycle is the cyclical movement of oxygen through the atmosphere, biosphere, and lithosphere, driven by the process of photosynthesis. Everything in nature cycles through different stages. Why would we expect our thoughts to be any different?

Yet, linear thinking prevents us from recognizing the cyclical nature of the creative process. This problem is not exclusive to creativity researchers. Just consider the ways that most new products are designed. The vast majority of engineers and inventors end their design process at the point of consumption or use. Essentially, they disregard half of the design challenge. Every product that is built, including the packaging, has to end up somewhere. What happens when the product stops functioning? If the design of that product does not include a means for disassembling it and reusing the parts or raw materials, then the design is incomplete and the product flawed. This design flaw pertains to virtually every product manufactured today, which is why our landfills are overflowing with garbage. The proliferation of garbage and industrial pollutants just confirms our lack of understanding, as a civilization, of the creation cycle.

Linear thinking also impacts our relationship to the aging process. Although we refer to the life span as a "life cycle," we fail to grasp its cyclical nature. The prevailing view in our society is that we grow and thrive for the first half of our lives and then undergo a steady decline leading to our deaths. But what if we had a truly cyclical view of the life span? Then we would realize that every developmental stage is a tradeoff, in which something is lost and something else is gained. As a society, we celebrate childbirth, but from the newborn's perspective, the birth experience is extremely traumatic. All at once, the infant is thrust into a noisy, chaotic world. The moment of birth marks both the beginning of an exciting and challenging new phase of existence and the end of an entirely different phase, in which every need has been met in an effortless manner. Just think of what the newborn has just given up: warmth, protection, nourishment, and nurturance, all provided by an unconditionally loving presence with an intuitive understanding of those needs.

Conversely, our youth-centered culture focuses on everything that is lost in the aging process: vigor, attractiveness, strength, agility, and mental acuity. Even our elders tend to buy into this view. Many find aging to be an unpleasantness to be endured. Towards the end of her life, actress Bette Davis is believed to have made this now-famous remark: "Old age ain't no place for sissies."[54]

Without denying the challenges of aging, we might at least consider the possibility that something valuable is being gained in this process. Typically, we see wisdom as a function of age. The problem is that wisdom is a hard thing to define—especially for the young. Researchers who study wisdom seem to define it in such a way as to reflect their own strengths and virtues. Early in my career, I conducted a research study with a group of students taking a course on personality psychology. I gave each student a list of 300 adjectives and 100 self-statements. They had to select the ones that: a) best described themselves, and b) best described someone they knew personally and considered wise.

Not surprisingly, the students perceived a great deal of similarity between themselves and their "wise" person. Yet there were seven statements they found applicable only to the other person but not to themselves. These statements, which reveal the essential characteristics of wisdom, are shown below:

1. The sensation of having access to a limitless source of energy.
2. Knowing that there is greatness in every person.
3. Knowing that you are more than just the sum of your parts.
4. The sensation of having no limits.
5. The feeling that there is an absolute truth.
6. A sense of belonging.
7. Feeling so calm that nothing can disturb you.

When looking at these seven statements, the most striking characteristic is the impression of being aligned with something much greater than oneself. Wise individuals appear to be aware of a core reality that is limitless and all-encompassing. Moreover, they recognize this infinite nature as something that exists within all things, including themselves. That is an important discovery. Although much is lost in the aging process, clearly something precious is gained, as well.

As psychiatrist Carl Jung observed, life has two phases, both of which are equally valuable. "The afternoon of life is just as full of meaning as the morning; only, its meaning and purpose are different." Jung viewed aging as a process of discovering what is most essential within oneself. "The privilege of a lifetime is to become who you really are."[55]

## Merging and Emerging

The biphasic nature of the life cycle reflects something essential about the creation cycle, as well. Here, we arrive at another key principle of Deep Creativity:

*Tenet #4: Creativity has two phases: merging and emerging.*

In the emerging phase, consciousness gives rise to the universal mind, which includes but is not limited to the individual mind and its contents. If creativity were a linear process, that would be the end of the story. But there is also a merging phase, which is equally important. In this phase, the universal mind and all of its contents merge back into consciousness.

The merging phase of the creation cycle cannot be overlooked. For new ideas and images to emerge, existing ways of thinking must be surrendered. In a very real sense, creation comes out of destruction, just as life comes out of death. Our society has a strong bias against death and destruction, at least as creative forces. But the Latin root of the word *destroy* (DE- and –STRUCT) just means "to undo. The act of creating is often about undoing. We may have to let go of certain presumptions to see things in a new light.

Just think of how technology evolves. Vinyl records give way to cassette tapes, which in turn are followed by CDs and then MP3 files. Each new innovation marks the end of an old technology. If you do not believe that creation comes out of destruction, try finding a cassette player in an electronics store. Old ways of thinking have to die off for new ones to take hold. That is the whole point of a paradigm shift.

We see the same pattern of merging and emerging throughout nature. Research on plate tectonics has shown that the plates making up the Earth's outermost shell emerge from the mantle at various hot spots and then merge back into the mantle through the process of subduction. Forest fires give rise to new growth; the heat from a fire opens the cones on pines, birch and spruce, causing the release of seeds that have been waiting for years to escape.

The creation cycle applies to everything. In *The Hero with a Thousand Faces*, Joseph Campbell points out that all mythology comes out of a fundamental understanding of this cyclical process. "The universal doctrine teaches that all the visible structures of the world—all things and all beings—are the effects of a ubiquitous power from which they arise, which supports and fills them during the period of their manifestation, and back into which they must ultimately dissolve."[56]

Deep Creativity relies on this universal doctrine. If our intention is to truly comprehend the creative process, we have no choice but to recognize its cyclical nature. Every thought emerges from consciousness, is sustained by it, and eventually merges back into it. In this cycle, thoughts emerge when the unity of consciousness shatters into multiplicity. These thoughts are contained within the universal mind and a tiny subset of them become accessible to each individual mind. Under the right conditions, all thoughts return to consciousness.

The creation cycle moves from consciousness to mind and then back again. Meditation practitioners learn to observe this process, noticing how individual thoughts emanate from consciousness and then dissolve back into it. This type of observation can lead to profound realizations, such as this one described by Sogyal Rinpoche:

> What happened in that astounding moment? Past thoughts had died away, the future had not yet arisen; the stream of my thoughts was cut right through. In that pure shock a gap opened, and in that gap was laid bare a sheer, immediate awareness of the present, one that was free of any clinging. It was simple, naked, and fundamental. And yet that naked simplicity was also radiant with the warmth of an immediate compassion.[57]

## Sleep and Dreams

You do not need to know a single thing about meditation to experience the creation cycle. In fact, you and I experience this cycle on a daily basis—or, more precisely, a nightly one. According to Campbell, the creation cycle "is to be understood as the passage of universal consciousness from the deep sleep zone of the unmanifest, through dream, to the full day of waking; then back again through dream to the timeless dark."[58]

We know that sleep is a cyclical process. Every night, we cycle through the various stages of sleep, progressing from lighter to deeper sleep, and then to the REM (rapid eye movement) stage, during which dreaming is most likely to occur. Carl Jung maintained that dream symbols are the product of the *collective unconscious*, which he defined as a part of the mind derived from ancestral memory and common to all human beings. In Deep Creativity, we see dreams as tapping into the universal mind, which is a more expansive notion, because: a) it is not limited to our ancestral history; and b) its contents are not necessarily unconscious.

The transition from waking to deep sleep allows our minds to merge into consciousness, from which the universal mind emerges during REM and then our individual minds coalesce as we awaken. Our minds are being regenerated every morning when we awaken from sleep, which means that our thought patterns may not be exactly the same as they were the night before. That is part of the reason why sleep can be so refreshing. We have the opportunity to let go of the past each night and to start over the next day. The person that awakens from sleep in the morning may differ in noticeable ways from the one that fell asleep the night before. If you go to bed angry or upset, often those emotions have shifted or dissipated by the time you awaken. The principle of "sleeping on it" when you have a tough decision to make or a problem to solve seems particularly sound. It gives you a chance at a clean slate and a fresh perspective.

When we sleep, we immerse ourselves in the creation cycle. This explains why sleep—and particularly dreams—can be such a fertile ground for creativity. The universal mind, which guides our dreams, encompasses the totality of human thought. In dreams, anything is possible. We can fly to other solar systems and galaxies, take different forms, hold conversations with plants and animals, and commune with loved ones long dead or not yet born. The universal mind has none of the restrictions that limit our individual minds. Its vantage point extends beyond the most distant horizons.

Throughout history, dramatic creative breakthroughs have taken place in dreams. René Descartes conceived of the ideas in his groundbreaking *Discourse on Method* through a series of dreams, one of which was actually a dream within a dream. Elias Howe invented the modern sewing machine in a dream. August Kekulé discovered the cyclical structure of benzene as a result of a dream image of a snake biting its own tail. Paul McCartney believed that the melody to "Yesterday" came to him in a dream. Samuel Taylor Coleridge claimed that he dreamed the entire poem "Xanadu," which is why the poem is subtitled, "A Vision in a Dream." Neils Bohr dreamed of a planetary system as a model for the atom—a notion for which he was awarded the 1922 Nobel Prize in physics. And Giuseppe Tartini composed his most well-known work, *The Devil's Sonata*, while dreaming that the devil was playing the piece for him.

Most of us know from direct experience that our dreams tend to be far more intricate and expansive than the fragments we are able to recall when we awaken. If the universal mind guides our dreams, and all thoughts exist within it, then our dreams should give us access to limitless possibilities. Yet we can only grasp the ideas and images that make sense to our individual minds. Each person's mind is masterful at detecting patterns, but only those patterns that it is prepared to receive.

This preparation has to do with a number of factors, including an individual's interests and passions; innate ability; upbringing; educational background; and societal and cultural influences. Clearly, a physicist is less likely to recall a dream symphony than a musician or composer would. To detect a musical pattern, it helps to have not just musical training but an ear for music. In other words, you are not going to hear music if you are not prepared to listen for it.

Those who experience creative breakthroughs in their dreams have devoted themselves to the pursuit of that particular type of breakthrough. Descartes had spent years contemplating the very questions that were answered in his dreams. Similarly, McCartney received the melody of "Yesterday" at the peak of the Beatles' productivity—a two-year period during which they toured the world, made films, recorded three of the most influential albums in the history of popular music, and wrote songs at a staggering pace.

The idea of preparation being critical to the creative process is far from new. But where Deep Creativity deviates from past approaches has to do with the function of that preparation. All of us have equal access to the universal mind, which contains every imaginable thought. Because of the specific directions each of us has chosen to take in our lives, we are uniquely prepared to detect certain patterns above all others. If we could expand our range of interests and proclivities, we might become fluent enough in the language of math, science, art, literature and music to detect notable patterns in all of them. What distinguishes a broad thinker like Leonardo da Vinci from the vast majority of creative individuals is his receptivity to ideas and images that were not confined to a single pursuit or discipline. This raises some intriguing questions regarding the limits of our own receptivity. If we opened our minds to new possibilities, what kinds of patterns might we be able to detect?

CHAPTER 6

# The Creative Emotions

*"God hid the whole world in thy heart."*
*—Ralph Waldo Emerson*

The entire cycle of creation is fueled by emotion. Intensity and passion have always driven the creative process. We see ample evidence of this in the reflections of artists:

> Fine works of art never age, because they are marked with genuine feeling. The language of the passions—the impulse of the heart—are always the same.
> —Eugene Delacroix[59]

> The artist knows the right moment, and also the relentless, tireless, depth-probing urge. The moment is a flashing spark, the relentless urge, the everlasting holy fire.
> —Emil Nolde[60]

> My work contains the whole soul of a man who has known
> the depths of life's mysteries, who has sought them as a lover,
> with joy, and reverence, and fear.
> —Pablo Picasso[61]

In *Outliers*, author Malcolm Gladwell introduced his "10,000-hour rule," which is the idea that world-class expertise in any field tends to come after 10,000 hours of effective practice.[62] To put this in perspective, if you practiced a particular skill 40 hours a week for 50 weeks a year, it would take you five years to reach the 10,000-hour milestone. That is an enormous commitment—one that relatively few of us are willing to make. It begs the question: What would possess someone to devote so much of their lives to a single pursuit?

Of course, we already know the answer: *Passion*. As the Italian scientist and mathematician, Galileo Galilei, so famously observed, "Passion is the genesis of genius."[63] According to Gladwell, individuals who earn the label of genius in some field of endeavor all have one thing in common; they are actively in love with the thing they do, in a manner that closely resembles romantic love. This intensity is captured beautifully in the words of Russian painter Ilya Repin, who once told an interviewer, "I love art more than virtue, more than people, more than family, more than friends, more than any happiness or joy in life. I love it secretly, jealously as an old drunkard—incurably."[64]

## Love and Joy

Creativity research has largely overlooked the power of intense emotion, which is at the heart of the creative process. Two emotions in particular—love and joy—drive this process. Each emotion corresponds to one of the two phases of the creation cycle. This gives rise to another fundamental idea:

*Tenet #5: Creative energy takes two forms:*
*Joy is the energy of emerging, and love is the energy of merging.*

Let us consider each of these emotions separately:

## Joy

In the emerging phase, consciousness shatters into the universal mind. It is joy that bursts open the perfect unity of pure consciousness and disperses it into myriad thought forms. I know this to be true from my own direct experience, which is confirmed by mystics throughout history. One of the central notions of Hinduism is captured in this line of verse from the Upanishads: "From joy all beings have come, by joy they all live, and unto joy they all return."[65] The Buddha taught, "When the mind is pure, joy follows like a shadow that never leaves."[66]

Joy is the radiant energy that transforms consciousness into ideas, images, and insights. Artists understand the profound link between joy and creative expression. "Art grows out of joy," claimed painter Edvard Munch.[67] According to adventurer Chris McCandless, "The joy of life comes from our encounters with new experiences."[68] William Wordsworth wrote, "With an eye made quiet by the power of harmony, and the deep power of joy, we see into the life of things."[69] With respect to education, Einstein maintained, "It is the supreme art of the teacher to awaken joy in creative expression."[70] William Butler Yeats observed that "all joyous or creative life is a re-birthing as something not oneself, something which has no memory and is created in a moment and perpetually renewed."[71]

American psychologist Rollo May had much to say about the role of joy in the creative process. In describing the experience of creative insight, he noted, "If only for that moment, we participate in the myths of creation. Order comes out of disorder, form out of chaos, as it did in the creation of the universe. The sense of joy comes from our participation, no matter how slight, in being as such."[72]

In these few words, May manages to convey the notion of the human being as a *microcosm*. The same creative process that gives rise to universes is also responsible for our individual creativity. This is because every level of being is contained within each of us, including the pure consciousness that represents the source of all creation and the universal mind that encompasses every thought.

Again, we turn to May, who explains: "Joy, rather than happiness, is the goal of life, for joy is the emotion which accompanies our fulfilling our natures as human beings."[73] In the experience of joy, we become, all at once: a) consciousness embedding itself within the universal mind; b) the individual thoughts within the universal mind that receive and carry consciousness; and c) the blast of energy that yields this profound transformation.

## Love

In the merging phase, individual thoughts give way to consciousness as the distinctions existing within the universal mind simply melt away. Love is the force that drives this transition. With love, all boundaries dissolve into perfect unity. Philosopher Emanuel Swedenborg wrote, "Love in its essence is spiritual fire."[74] While the fire may be purifying, it is ultimately destructive. In the presence of love, any sense of separateness ceases to exist.

In Matthew 10:34, Jesus alludes to the destructive nature of love. "Do not think I have come to bring peace to the world," he asserts. "I came not to bring peace, but a sword." For many, this passage is a source of discomfort. It gives the impression of Jesus as violent and divisive, especially when followed by these words. "For I came to set a man against his father, and a daughter against her mother, and a daughter-in-law against her mother-in-law; and a man's enemies will be members of his household."

Then, the next verse makes Jesus seem almost egomaniacal. "He who loves father or mother more than Me is not worthy of Me; and he who loves son or daughter more than Me is not worthy of Me." Jesus is actually speaking to the true nature of love. His message of love is revolutionary in terms of its inclusiveness. When it comes to love, says Jesus, there can be no distinction between friend and enemy, or beloved and stranger. The love he envisions exists only in the absence of such boundaries. Unless your love applies to everyone and everything equally, it is not really love, according to Jesus. That is why he challenges us to cast the net of our love as far as it can reach: "Anyone who welcomes you welcomes me, and anyone who welcomes me welcomes the one who sent me."[75]

The French writer, La Rochefoucauld, observed, "True love is like ghosts, which everyone talks about and few have seen."[76] To know love is to recognize its capacity to destroy everything. Love acts as a universal solvent that dissolves all thoughts, including our concept of the self. Immersed in love, our sense of personal identity disappears, as the lines between *self* and *other* become blurred. In a very real sense, love is lethal. Each of us ceases to exist as a separate entity when we have surrendered completely to love.

## Emotion and Creative Energy

Through the emotions of love and joy, we experience the energy that propels the creative process forward. Most creativity researchers are reluctant to make any mention of creative energy, even though they know that every creative process has an energetic component. The reason for this reluctance has to do with a strange dichotomy that seems to exist regarding energy—at least in the minds of many researchers. In the context of physics and chemistry, energy appears to be a legitimate scientific construct that can be measured with the greatest precision. But in the context of psychology, energy seems insubstantial and vague. Researchers who dare to mention creative energy run the risk of being discredited and having their ideas dismissed as pseudoscience.

This is why one of the most respected scientists in this field wrote an entire book on a creative experience he called "flow," without every daring to address this very basic question: *What is flowing in "flow?"*[77] For most of us, the answer to this question would be obvious: It *has* to be energy. All flow is energetic. Whether we are talking about the flow of water in a stream or of ideas in our minds, the driving force is energy. Even the most reductive scientists are willing to link thought processes to the flow of nerve impulses in the brain, and those impulses are simply the transmission of chemical and electrical energy.

For over half a century, psychologists have accepted the idea that emotions have two components: physiological arousal and a psychological interpretation of that arousal. The arousal part of emotion is something with which you are already very familiar: Your heart races, your palms get sweaty, your blood pressure increases, and you begin to hyperventilate. Arousal is an increase in your physical energy levels, which means that emotions boil down to energy.

How your mind interprets the arousal depends on a number of factors, including the context in which this energy boost occurs. Ultimately, your mind assigns a label to the arousal, calling it happiness, fear, anger, excitement or any number of other emotions. How you interpret the arousal is entirely up to you. In most cases, the arousal is the same.

*Love* and *joy* are the labels we have assigned to the energy associated with the creation cycle. In one phase, the contents of the universal mind emerge from consciousness in a burst of joy, and in the other, those contents merge back into consciousness, carried by a stream of love. In reality, love and joy are simply two sides of the same coin. The main difference we can detect between them has to do with the function each one carries out. Love leads to communion with the source of all creation, whereas joy makes it possible for that source to generate new possibilities.

## Bliss and Ecstasy

In the creation cycle, love and joy are inseparable. Both contribute in important ways to the creative experience. Together, they give rise to new types of emotional experiences. One of those experiences is bliss; the other is ecstasy. Both are compound emotions consisting of love and joy. And both are critical to the creative process.

The difference between bliss and ecstasy is partly one of intensity. In bliss, we melt into pure consciousness; in ecstasy, we explode. The creation cycle, in essence, has two volume settings, both of which are equally compelling. In gentler moments, we experience the sensation of bliss, which the dictionary defines as "a state of perfect happiness, typically so as to be oblivious of everything else." As the intensity increases, we may experience ecstasy, which is defined as "an overwhelming feeling of great happiness or joyful excitement."[78]

Both emotions lead to the merging of our minds into the unity of consciousness. From there, all things become possible. We can never underestimate the creative power of these emotions. The Upanishads remind us of their expansiveness:

> As great as the infinite space beyond is the space within
> the lotus of the heart. Both heaven and earth are contained in
> that inner space, both fire and air, sun and moon, lightning

and stars. Whether we know it in this world or know it not, everything is contained in that inner space.[79]

The only thing that differs between bliss and ecstasy is the way we access our vast creative power. When we are in bliss, we experience the merging of our individual minds into the pure formless essence of consciousness. In ecstasy, our mind expands into the universal mind first. It is no longer a single perspective merging into consciousness, but rather an infinite number. Ecstasy shatters us into a million pieces, each of which finds its way back to the source.

Bliss starts with love, whereas ecstasy starts with joy. Love is the energy of merging into consciousness; joy is the energy that accompanies the emergence of the universal mind. Our individual minds happen to be a gateway to both. We can enter the creation cycle from the standpoint of either consciousness or the universal mind. Why is that? One reason is that we are a microcosm. Both consciousness and the universal mind abide in us, without a doubt. But the individual mind is a gateway because it also happens to be a walled city. We have built a wall that has excluded so very much from the purview of the self. Just beyond that wall, the entire cycle of creation is taking place at this very moment. Fortunately for us, there is a gateway to the other side. The gate within the mind opens in response to love, joy, ecstasy and bliss. The powerful energy of these emotions acts like a gust of wind that blows the gate wide open.

## Which Comes First?

Creative breakthroughs are often accompanied by the emotions of bliss and ecstasy. Researchers commonly assume that the breakthrough comes first, and that the emotions follow. But what if it were the other way around? Could it be that the breakthrough is actually the consequence and not the cause of these emotions? Regarding this issue, Rollo May has observed:

> When my insight suddenly breaks through—which may happen when I am chopping wood in the afternoon—I experience a strange lightness in my step as though a great load were taken off my shoulders, a sense of joy on a deeper level that

continues without any relation whatever to the mundane tasks that I may be performing at the time. It cannot be just that the problem at hand has been answered—that generally brings only a sense of relief. What is the source of this curious pleasure?[80]

May recognizes that the insight itself would only evoke a sense of relief. At that moment, creative tension is alleviated and whatever caused that tension has been resolved. Yet, there seems to be something else at play here. The experience includes other, more powerful emotions. Feelings of bliss and ecstasy actually precede and give rise to the creative breakthrough.

I know this to be the case because I have observed it in myself on numerous occasions. When I experience these emotions, I find myself drawn entirely into the creation cycle. At such moments, my mind dissolves into pure consciousness, and I am unaware of anything beyond the experience I am having then and there. In fact, I lose myself in the moment. This is not hyperbole; my self-awareness literally disappears, and I cease to exist as anything other than the experience itself.

That is when I gain the greatest clarity. It is as if I can see every thought pattern arising from consciousness, all at once, as the universal mind emerges. Imagine having all the world's treasures laid out in front of you and being granted permission to take whatever you can carry. There is only one catch, though; you cannot use any kind of container. You can only take whatever you can hold in your arms.

In this case, I feel that I have gained momentary access to a treasure trove of knowledge, which is magnificent in its expansiveness. What I bring back from this experience is limited by my mind's capacity to grasp the concepts and visions that present themselves to me. Usually, the insights that "stick" are related to whatever issues I have been contemplating in the recent past. My mind is predisposed to attend to specific thought patterns while disregarding the rest. Psychologists call this predisposition *set*, referring to the set of expectations that shape our experience by making us particularly sensitive to certain types of information.

I know that I am more sensitive to some ideas relative to others because my entire life history has prepared me to be. Everything that has come before has shaped and colored my mind, determining the thought patterns to which I am most likely to be receptive. My entire adult life has been devoted to understanding human consciousness and its role in the creative process. That is why my own personal creative breakthroughs do not pertain to quantum theory or microeconomics. I am simply not oriented towards those concerns.

By drawing us into the creation cycle, the experience of bliss or ecstasy gives us access to limitless knowledge. We are able to transition from our own individual minds to the realms of consciousness and the universal mind. In doing so, we participate in the eternal dance of creation that gives rise to all things, including our own thoughts. Although the source of these thoughts is limitless, our individual minds are not. We can only grasp what we are prepared to grasp. Everything else must fall away. But the creative process expands us, so that with every new discovery and insight, our range of understanding broadens. This is the beauty of a life devoted to a creative pursuit.

## CHAPTER 7

# The Creative Trinity

*"The best things in life come in threes, like friends, dreams, and memories."*
*—Mencius*

So far, we have looked at the various elements of creativity individually. Now we begin to see how those elements come together. This will give us a fresh understanding of the creative process, yield insights into our own creative abilities, and show us how those abilities can be enhanced.

In many of the world's mystical traditions, the essential nature of reality is threefold. We see this in the Christian trinity: Father, Son, and Holy Spirit. Tibetan Buddhist teachings describe three realms: *Dharmakaya, Nirmanakaya*, and *Sambhogakaya*. In Hinduism, there is an ultimate, unchanging reality that can be experienced as the interrelationship of three components: *sat* (manifestation), *chit* (consciousness), and *ananda* (bliss).

A number of scholars have compared these different triads and pointed out their commonalities. The Christian notion of the Father seems to align with the Hindu *chit* and the Buddhist *Dharmakaya*, all of which identify the pure consciousness from which all things arise. In each of these traditions, there is also a mediating energy (Holy Spirit, *ananda*, *Sambhogakaya*), resulting in the tangible manifestation of consciousness in the realm of matter and thought (Son, *sat*, *Nirmanakaya*).

From the perspective of Deep Creativity, these triads offer important insights into the nature of the creative process. To help us understand this process more fully, we will consider the following principle:

### Tenet #6: The three elements of creativity are: Creator, creating, and creation.

Here, we encounter the idea of a *creative trinity*. In the creative process, three elements come together. Each of these is important in its own right. Together, they open us up to a realm of limitless possibility.

## Creator

The first of these is the Creator, which corresponds largely to the realm of consciousness. This is the source of all thoughts and all things. As we have seen, the Creator can be considered the interplay of being and non-being, although it ultimately defies description. Having no limits of any kind, the Creator exists beyond any mental representation we try to impose on it. We can only know it through direct experience. Any attempt to comprehend the Creator conceptually is destined to fall short.

We know the Creator exists because of our own experience of it, as well as the accounts of mystics and artists that have attempted to share their own moments of communion. Knowledge of the Creator is not a matter of faith. If you have had such moments, there is no room for doubt. And if you have not, there is nothing that can or should convince you.

All of our thoughts emerge from the Creator. The creative process shatters the perfect unity of the Creator, and when this happens, consciousness becomes embedded in each individual thought. If the Creator can be thought of as the eternal dance of being and non-being—unity and void—then this dance is proliferated within every thought that arises from it.

The very notion of a Creator lies at the core of Deep Creativity, and I realize that it may be deeper than some of you may want to go. You are hoping to gain an understanding of the creative process that will perhaps allow you to enhance your own creativity. But you are not necessarily trying to find religion here.

The language I have chosen does seem suspiciously religious. Why, after all, do we need to have a "Creator" with a capital *C*? My answer is that there is only one. If you accept the tenets of Deep Creativity, then you recognize that the single source of all human creativity is the pure consciousness of what I am calling the Creator. Your own creativity relies ultimately on your ability to align yourself as much as possible with this consciousness. You can try using your mind exclusively to create, by dividing one thought into two or combining two thoughts into one, and this approach will perhaps bear some fruit. But the enormous breakthroughs and revelations that shatter existing paradigms and give rise to entirely new ways of being and looking at the world require an altogether different approach. If you seek to illuminate or transcend the mysteries of the universe, you are destined to enter the realm of the Creator.

This is a realm of pure being, pure experience. The only thing that can keep you from it is the activity of your own mind. As Rumi wrote, "No mind, no intellect can penetrate the mystery of His unending state."[81] This is because the Creator has no limits—not even space or time. Our minds can only grasp the limited, not the limitless. We require boundaries and edges giving rise to detectable patterns so that we can know where one thing ends and the next begins. Without the ability to draw such distinctions, we would never be able to organize, categorize, and make sense of our world.

Creativity that inspires and revolutionizes rarely begins with a thought, but rather an experience. Circumstances trigger a feeling of connection with something greater than oneself, which is both profound and mysterious. "The most important function of art and science," claimed Einstein, "is to awaken this feeling and keep it alive."[82]

Given that all creating is becoming, the only way to create is through direct experience. You can only become something by experiencing it first-hand. And the only way to do that is by aligning yourself with the Creator, which is the pure consciousness through which all experience can be known. The bold idea here is that there is only one consciousness, one experiencer, one Creator. Although the Creator permeates all things—including you and me—our minds can create the illusion of separateness. The creative process demands that we transcend the limitations of our minds as well as this illusion of separateness.

In other words, if we want to be creative, we have to align ourselves with the Creator. This means merging into pure consciousness, which is the source of all thoughts and all things. From that vantage point, we can become, and thereby create, virtually anything we want. We just need to know how to engage fully in the creative process.

## Creating

In Deep Creativity, our focus is on the creative process. Without this process, the consciousness of the Creator does not yield anything new. The act of creating is the vehicle that drives creativity. Here is what we already know about this act:

All creating is becoming. In the creative process, the pure consciousness of the Creator gets embedded into new thoughts and eventualities. As we have seen, creating is a cyclical process consisting of two phases: merging and emerging. In the emerging phase, the perfect unity of the Creator is shattered in ways that give rise to an infinite array of thoughts. These thoughts, which make up the universal mind, are simply patterns of binary code: 1's and 0's, being and non-being, unity and void.

A subset of this code is accessible to each individual mind. Our mind's ability to detect thought patterns depends on a host of variables, including genetic and environmental factors. But when this mind merges back into the Creator, we return to the source of all thought, and in so doing, we expand our mental capacity infinitely. Just like the emerging phase, the act of merging into the Creator is transformative. We become the Creator—the origin and essence of all thought.

Here, you will find a radical idea: We create the Creator within ourselves during the merging phase, simply by becoming one with pure consciousness. Do you realize how revolutionary this is? It implies that to a certain extent, the source of all our thought is something we create! In the process of creating, we embed the

Creator in our own minds. Without this step, nothing else can take place because all of our creativity emerges from a source that has to exist within us.

The entire process is driven by energy. We have already seen that creative energy comes in two forms: love and joy. In the emerging phase of the creation cycle, the unity of the Creator shatters into the myriad forms that make up creation, driven by the power of joy. And in the merging phase, it is love that brings it all back together, returning whatever has been created back to its source.

Through joy, the Creator gives itself entirely to creation by embedding itself in every thought. Through love, the Creator receives each thought back into itself by allowing all distinctions to melt away. Love unites and joy divides. Both are essential to the creative process.

Either of these emotions can serve as an entryway into the creative process. Simply by experiencing them, you generate the energy that propels the creation cycle onward. This cycle revolves around the Creator. So, when you immerse yourself in love or joy, you align yourself with the source of all creation.

## Creation

The act of creating results in creation. This seemingly obvious statement carries great power. Although Deep Creativity places emphasis on the creative process, we also recognize that this process cannot be understood without looking at the nature of creative products.

If the creative process were linear, then the creation—the ultimate product that emerges from this process—would be the end point. In a results-oriented society, we are greatly invested in the products of human creativity. We seek new ideas, breakthroughs, and innovations that can solve global problems, enhance our quality of life, and serve the needs of humanity, while also yielding greater market share, acclaim, and power.

But what do we actually know about these creative products? In Deep Creativity, we recognize that the creative process is not linear, and so there can be no final product. Everything that gets created is the starting point for something else. Ideas are constantly evolving, as are the situations in which they get applied. Yesterday's breakthrough becomes today's status quo and tomorrow's history lesson. Every shiny new gizmo that comes off an assembly line ends up tarnished, broken, or obsolete. Just think about that kitchen you plan to remodel. The fixtures, appliances, flooring, countertops and backsplash that now seem so outdated were once considered "state-of-the-art." At some point in the past, green refrigerators and yellow stoves were all the rage. Yes, that's right. Someone actually chose them in a showroom and felt great pride in owning such beautiful, modern conveniences.

We also know that all of creation can be broken down into two classes: thoughts and things. Thoughts are created "in here," within our own minds, whereas things are created "out there," in the world at large. Obviously, this distinction has its limits. For instance, we know that virtually every*thing* created by a human being starts off as a *thought*. Great inventors often envision their devices completely in their mind's eye before they ever put pencil to paper or begin the fabrication process.

Thoughts can give rise to other thoughts (as in logical inference) or to things (the tangible products of our creativity). Similarly, things can give rise to other things (an earthquake resulting in a tsunami) or to thoughts (a lightning storm inspiring a creative breakthrough). The distinction between thoughts and things can become very blurred for one simple reason: We are not always able to tell where "out there" ends and "in here" begins.

As we have already seen, the universal mind encompasses all thoughts. This includes anything that you or I can conceive with our individual minds. But it also includes all *things*, because every phenomenon or object that we can perceive or imagine exists only as a thought—at least to us. The entire universe lives within the mind of the individual that apprehends it. When we think of something, there is no way to separate the thing from our thought of it.

You are probably very familiar with this riddle: "If a tree falls in the forest and no one is around to hear it, does it make a sound?" In response to this thought experiment, philosopher George Berkeley wrote, "The objects of sense exist only when they are perceived; the trees therefore are in the garden no longer than while there is somebody by to perceive them."[83]

Whether or not Berkeley was right, one thing is clear: We can never prove the existence of anything independently of ourselves. How do we know that the tree even exists when we are not there to think about it? Of course, the answer is that we can never know—at least not with any kind of certainty.

But we do know that anything we can call to mind has to exist within our thoughts, whether or not it has an independent existence "out there." If the universal mind encompasses all thoughts, then it must also encompass all things. The term *creation* refers to both. All of creation is imbued with the pure consciousness of the Creator. As we know, consciousness embeds itself at every level of creation, resulting in a fractal universe.

Although we think of ourselves as an infinitesimal part of creation, the Creator is fully present in us. There is a rich, multifaceted universe within each of us. Consciousness does not simply permeate us but also every cell in our body, not to mention the molecules that make up those cells, and the atoms and subatomic particles within each molecule. Looking closely at our own bodies, we see universes nested within universes.

But on the mental level, each of us tends to limit ourselves to the confines of our own individual mind. This limitation appears to be completely arbitrary. The sum total of what we have thought until now is a miniscule portion of what we are capable of thinking. Beyond the confines of our tiny little minds lies a vast field of possibility. The entirety of creation, including all thoughts and all things, unfolds within the realm of the universal mind, and each of us has access to the whole—at least theoretically.

The reason we do not stray from the familiar is that we are living in a prison cell of our own making. These little minds of ours have served us quite well in most regards, helping us survive and perhaps even thrive in a world that poses constant challenges to our safety, security, and stability. But they also tend to lock us in place, creating habits and routines that we somehow feel compelled to maintain. If you have ever thought your life was drudgery, then you may also appreciate the irony in the fact that you have made a daily choice to live in this manner.

In actuality, our lives are an improvisation. When we take a step in a particular direction, we tend to disregard the fact that we could have gone in any number of other directions. Whether we choose to recognize it or not, we have 360 degrees of possibilities at our disposal.

You may be thinking: *I don't really have any choices. My responsibilities limit what I can and cannot do.* To which I would reply with a simple question: How did you assume those responsibilities? I realize that the decisions we make and the burdens we carry have a complex history. The circumstances of our lives have led us to this point. Yet, we are not slaves to anything other than our own expectations. Whatever traps we have fallen into are the ones we have set for ourselves.

The whole of creation can be found in the individual that has managed to escape these self-imposed traps. The person who can transcend the limits of the individual mind discovers a core identity which is connected to everything. For the artist, this discovery may only last a moment or two. The artist may tap into the universal mind just long enough to gain a bit of clarity, catch glimpses of wholeness, and extract a few precious insights.

For the mystic, however, the idea is to remain in this expanded state. Rumi wrote:

> I am the life of life.
> I am that cat, this stone, no one.
> I have thrown duality away like an old dishrag,
> I see and know all times and worlds,
> As one, one, always one.[84]

Mystics journey into the heart of creation in order to experience a sense of communion. Creativity is not the primary concern. This is not to say that mystics cannot express themselves creatively. In fact, Rumi left behind some of the most beautiful and inspiring poetry ever written. But we get a sense, when reading his poetry, that his intention was to provide hints and clues to the experience of an ineffable mystery. Although the essence of this experience can never be captured in words, enough of the feeling can be conveyed by Rumi's poetry to help open doors for others.

At their core, the mystical experience and the creative process share an important quality. Both result in the expansion of the mind. In its most expanded form, the individual mind gives way to the universal mind, which holds all of creation. "The nature of mind is the nature of everything," wrote Dudjom Rinpoche.[85] In the Tibetan Buddhist trinity, the realm of manifestation, known as the *Nirmanakaya*, is often symbolized in the form of Padmasambhava, the eighth-century master who helped bring Buddhism to Tibet. What is the significance of this?

Among certain Tibetan Buddhist practitioners, Padmasambhava is seen as an embodiment of self-realization. He represents the latent capacity within each of us to align ourselves with the universal mind, and therefore with all of creation. When the creature that we are learns to identify with the Creator abiding within us, we human beings come into our own as creative agents.

## Creator-creating-creation

The Creator cannot simply reside in the formless realm of consciousness. We know that the consciousness of the Creator abides in all thoughts and all things. This is the realm of form that comprises the universal mind. Only when this mind emerges from consciousness can the Creator take form. So, the Creator must have two aspects: One transcendent and the other immanent. The Creator is embedded in all thoughts and things but must also transcend them. We acknowledged this at the outset when we observed that the ultimate source of all limited form must be limitless in nature.

The Creator has to exist as both consciousness and mind. At the same time, it must be divisible and indivisible, taking form while remaining formless. This seems paradoxical only because our minds are bound to distinctions and limitations that have an imperfect correspondence to reality. We cannot begin to comprehend the transcendent nature of the Creator with minds that have no way of dealing with something that can encompass nothing and everything at the same time; that is both limitless and limited; that is timeless yet impermanent; and that creates everything and nothing.

And what about the process of creating? If the Creator exists as both consciousness and mind, should it not also be found in the dynamic that transforms one into the other? The three aspects of the creative trinity are linked so closely that it would be impossible to separate any of them from the others. That is why, when we refer to the Creator, we are really talking about the *Creator-*

*creating-creation.* Within this trinity we find pure consciousness, universal mind, and the creative energy of love and joy. The three elements of the trinity are inseparable.

Each of us has the capacity to expand into the universal mind, merge into pure consciousness, and be filled with love and joy, thus assuming our rightful place as the Creator-creating-creation. We can embody the creative trinity as the entire creation cycle unfolds within us. This is our destiny, but only if we are willing to take bold leaps into the unknown, surrender the comfort of what is familiar, and undertake the ultimate adventure.

# CHAPTER 8

# The Creative Adventure

*"Get free. Be who you're supposed to be."*
*—Lauryn Hill*

L et's review: All of creation, including human creativity, arises from the Creator. Through the creation cycle, the universal mind emerges from consciousness and eventually merges back it. Although this limited mind of ours contains only the tiniest fraction of the thoughts available to the universal mind, it is also the starting point for all of our creativity.

So, how do we get from Point A to Point B? After all, the individual mind is far removed from the expansiveness of the Creator. If all creativity emerges from this unified source, then that should be the starting point of the creative process. Yet, we have no choice but to initiate the process from the narrow confines of our individual minds. That may seem less than ideal, but it represents one of the great and exciting challenges facing us as human beings. To tap into the true source of our creativity, we have to find a way to escape the limitations of our own minds. There is no other way to gain access to the creation cycle.

65

Most of us enter the creation cycle accidentally, without effort or intention. But for many artists, the process is far more deliberate. Perhaps one of the most unique qualities of human beings is our capacity to decide if and when we participate in the creation cycle. Each time we make this decision, it takes an element of courage, because in doing so, we relinquish our thoughts and our own self-concept. Even if we only let go for the briefest of moments, it feels a little like death.

Now imagine what it takes to devote one's life to a creative pursuit. This is an act of heroism. As a young graduate student, Joseph Campbell made a decision that changed the course of his life. When his university advisor tried to restrict his work to a narrow academic curriculum, Campbell said, "To hell with it," dropped out of school and pursued his own course of study. Regarding this decision, he later wrote:

> It takes courage to do what you want. Other people have
> a lot of plans for you. Nobody wants you to do what you want
> to do. They want you to go on their trip, but you can do what
> you want. I did. I went into the woods and read for five years.[86]

In 1949, Campbell published his first book, *The Hero with a Thousand Faces*, in which he traced the adventures of the hero as recounted in the mythological stories of every culture. A hero, according to Campbell, is an individual who "has found or done something beyond the normal range of achievement and experience...someone who has given his or her life to something bigger than oneself."[87] In the prototypical story, the hero breaks free of the limits of the conventional world, crossing the boundary into "a field that's unprotected, novel," and thus beginning a series of adventures that leads to a valuable discovery.[88] This discovery and the rewards that come with it are shared by the hero once the adventures are complete and the hero has returned home.

Campbell reminds us that all "mythology is poetry, it is metaphorical."[89] The symbols contained within the hero myth represent the central issues and stages found in the creative adventure of each individual. Just as the hero's adventures require that he or she "battle past...personal and local historical limitations to the generally valid, normally human forms,"[90] our personal creative adventure requires us to escape the limits of our own minds in order to assume the vantage point of the Creator, which is the one and only source of new ideas, images, and insights. Both processes share the same objective, which is to experience and create something fresh and transcendent. As Campbell explains, "A legendary hero is usually the founder of something—the founder of a new age, the founder of a new religion, the founder of a new city, the founder of a new way of life. In order to found something new, one has to leave the old and go in quest of the seed idea, a germinal idea that will have the potentiality of bringing forth that new thing."[91]

Not only are the trials and revelations of the hero metaphorical but even the very concept of the hero can be viewed as a symbol. If you look closely at this symbol you will find a thinly-veiled description of an artist. For instance, Campbell identifies the hero as someone who undergoes a profound transformation resulting in "visions, ideas, and inspirations (emerging) from the primary springs of human life and thought."[92] Compare that to the following statements made by artists about their own place in society:

> All civilizations and culture are the results of the creative imagination or artistic quality in man. The artist is the man who makes life more interesting or beautiful, more understandable or mysterious, or probably, in the best sense, more wonderful. His trade is to deal with illimitable experience.
> —George Bellows[93]

> Artists to my mind are the real architects of change, and not the legislators who implement change after the fact.
> —William Burroughs[94]

> The artist must create a spark before he can make a fire and before art is born, the artist must be ready to be consumed by the fire of his creation.
> —Auguste Rodin[95]

Every production of an artist should be the expression of an adventure of his soul.

—W. Somerset Maugham[96]

Who but the artist has the power to open man up, to set free the imagination? The others—priest, teacher, saint, statesman, warrior—hold us to the path of history. They keep us chained to the rock, so that the vultures may eat out our hearts. It is the artist who has the courage to go against the crowd; he is the unrecognized "hero of our time"—and of all time.

—Henry Miller[97]

In *The Hero with a Thousand Faces*, Campbell offers the following overview of the hero's mythological adventure: "A hero ventures forth from the world of common day into a region of supernatural wonder: fabulous forces are there encountered and a decisive victory is won: the hero comes back from this mysterious adventure with the power to bestow boons on his fellow man."[98] Compare this to the creative process: The artist ventures beyond the limits of the mind and into the realm of the Creator, where the ultimate creative forces are encountered and new ideas are discovered. The artist returns from the experience with the power to illuminate or transcend the mysteries of life.

In his comparative studies of hero myths, Campbell found three stages of a hero's adventures: Departure, Initiation, and Return. I will show you how these stages pertain to the creative process. The trials and revelations that the hero undergoes during each stage are symbolic of the transformative experiences familiar to most artists. This leads us to the next important principle of Deep Creativity:

*Tenet #7: The creative process is a heroic adventure consisting of three stages: Departure, Initiation, and Return.*

Over the next three chapters, we will explore each of these stages.

# CHAPTER 9

# Departure

*"Only those who will risk going too far can possibly find out how far one can go."*

—*T. S. Eliot*

In the hero myth, the Departure stage represents a separation from routine existence, from the safely marked highways associated with the conventional world. Before the adventure can truly begin, the hero must cross a threshold into the unknown. "The usual person is more than content, he is even proud, to remain within the indicated bounds, and popular belief gives him every reason to fear so much as the first step into the unexplored."[99] The hero, on the other hand, is compelled to cross over, into the realm of darkness and mystery where the adventures await. Three forces lead the hero into the heart of the adventure.

The first is the *Call to Adventure*, which signifies that "destiny has summoned the hero and transferred his spiritual center of gravity from within the pale of his society to a zone unknown."[100] Only someone who actually heeds the call can be considered a true hero. The summons can be ignored or rejected. In fact, the hero stands out because of his or her willingness to accept a challenge that the vast majority of people would refuse.

The second force that leads the hero to action is the guidance received from a figure representing "the benign, protecting power of destiny."[101] This figure serves as a mentor or guide, pointing the hero in the appropriate direction and providing the hero with the resources needed to pursue the adventure. The guide can take a feminine form—the fairy godmother, Virgin, or helpful crone—or a masculine one: "In fairy lore, it may be some little fellow of the wood, some wizard, hermit, shepherd, or smith, who appears, to supply the amulets and advice that the hero will require."[102]

Finally, the hero is compelled to act for the sake of liberating the flow of something valuable—a treasure that has been locked away and prevented from reaching the world. According to Campbell, this flow is the *life force* that "may be represented in physical terms as a circulation of food substance, dynamically as a streaming of energy, or spiritually as a manifestation of grace."[103] The source of this life force is consciousness itself, which Campbell calls the *World Navel*. "The torrent pours from an invisible source, the point of entry being the center of the symbolic circle of the universe, the Immovable Spot of the Buddha legend, around which the world may be said to revolve...Thus the World Navel is the symbol of the continuous creation: the mystery of the maintenance of the world through that continuous miracle of vivification which wells within all things."[104]

In symbolic form, the Departure stage of the hero's journey describes the initial phase of the creative process. We are seeking an entry point into the creation cycle. This cycle alternates between consciousness and the universal mind. Neither is a suitable entry point because each requires too big a leap. After all, how are we supposed to expand our tiny little minds to take in an entire universe of possibilities? Like most things in life, the creative process requires a gradual transition. We cannot go from 0 to 100 without gaining a bit of momentum first.

That is why the most suitable entry point is the very act of creating. When we considered the creative trinity—Creator-creating-creation—we discovered that the driving force for the act of creating can be found in the emotions of love and joy. In combination, these two emotions yield bliss and ecstasy. Both of those compound emotions act like rocket fuel for the creative process. It is the intensity of bliss and ecstasy, more than anything else, which allows an individual mind to gain access to the creation cycle.

In his own life, Campbell came up with a simple guiding principle that reflects this idea: *Follow your bliss*. When asked about the origins of this principle, he offered the following explanation:

> I came to this idea of bliss because in Sanskrit, which is the great spiritual language of the world, there are three terms that represent the brink, the jumping-off place to the ocean of transcendence: *sat, cit, ananda*. The word "sat" means being. "Chit" means consciousness. "Ananda" means bliss or rapture. I thought, "I don't know whether my consciousness is proper consciousness or not; I don't know whether what I know of my being is my proper being or not; but I do know where my rapture is. So let me hang onto rapture, and that will bring me both my consciousness and my being." I think it worked.[105]

We can perform a similar analysis of the creative trinity. Our individual minds can never fully comprehend the Creator, which extends far beyond the scope of our limited thought processes. And the vast expanses of creation, including all of the thoughts that we have yet to grasp, remain an intractable mystery to us. The one thing we can hold onto, in our creative pursuits, is the set of powerful emotions that fill our hearts: love and joy, bliss and ecstasy.

When we tap into these emotions, we begin to release the vast streams of energy that are needed to drive our creative process. It takes energy to break free of the tiny prison cell in which we have been locked away. This is the prison of our own thoughts. Ironically, we built the prison, and we are simultaneously its warden, prison guard, and inmate. Liberation is not easy. We have to build momentum to escape the gravitational pull of our habits, judgments, expectations, beliefs, and concepts—especially our self-concept.

## The Call to Adventure

The way we gain momentum is through circumstances that appear to be outside our control. In the Call to Adventure, such circumstances unfold in a manner that inspires us and brings us into direct contact with our own passion. For two young brothers living in a remote area of Brazil, the Call to Adventure took the form of a guitar they discovered one day in the jungle outside their village. They practiced together on the one guitar, learning how to play two parts simultaneously and eventually becoming one of Latin America's most popular recording acts: *Los Indios Tabajaras*.

The Call to Adventure can be a traumatic event. In the case of John Lennon and Paul McCartney, both men lost their mothers during their teen years, and both responded to their respective loss by immersing themselves in music. Lennon later observed that music "was the only thing that could get through to me after all the things that were happening when I was fifteen."[106] McCartney's brother recalled that Paul took up the guitar after his mother's death and "didn't have time to eat or think about anything else. He played it on the lavatory, in the bath, everywhere."[107]

Whatever form it may take, the Call to Adventure opens a potential door into the creative process. No two people are going to respond to the same situation in identical ways. What one person sees as a tragedy may strike another as an opportunity. When a fire destroyed Thomas Edison's laboratory, including all of his life's work and the prototypes of new inventions, he told his son, "It's all right. We've just got rid of a lot of rubbish."[108] Later, at the scene of the fire, Edison was quoted as saying, "I'll start over again tomorrow."[109]

The next day, while looking over the ruins, Edison remarked, "There is great value in disaster. All our mistakes are burned up. Thank God we can start anew."[110] Just as he had promised, Edison began rebuilding. Over the following year, his company generated 10 times as much in revenue as the net damages caused by the fire.[111]

In his response to the fire, Edison demonstrated a clear grasp of the heroic nature of the creative adventure. Although none of us may be able to control the things that happen in our lives, we have complete autonomy regarding our response to those events. Edison was able to look past the devastation and see an opportunity: the start of the next phase in his creative life. Whereas most people would have focused on the loss, Edison looked at the conflagration almost admiringly. He even called other members of his family to join him in witnessing it.

When the Call to Adventure arrives, we may not recognize it as such. How can we know that this particular event is an opportunity to embark on our creative adventure? There has to be a way to distinguish it from all the other events in our lives. The Call to Adventure may take a dramatic form, just to get our attention. Sometimes, we are put in a situation where we just have to choose. Every life has key turning points, when difficult decisions must be made. The heroic choice is to go in the direction that moves and inspires us, regardless of the consequences. What makes this choice so heroic is that there are *always* consequences. In pursuing our creative adventure, we may sacrifice any number of things, including security and stability. The temptation to play it safe can be very compelling.

In his analysis of hero myths, Joseph Campbell uncovered a variation of the hero myth in which the would-be hero chooses not to answer the Call to Adventure. "Refusal of the summons," he observes, "converts the adventure into its negative. Walled in boredom, hard work, or 'culture,' the subject loses the power of significant affirmative action and becomes a victim to be saved."[112]

What if you fail to act on the Call to Adventure? Campbell would argue that this is a common occurrence. Most of us are either unable to recognize the Call or unwilling to act upon it. This is why hero myths are so exciting. The hero does something bold and unusual, making decisions and acting in ways that most people would not. While the most common response to certain challenges is to play it safe, the hero chooses to go in a very different direction.

The same is true of artists. How rare is the person who will dedicate his or her life to a creative pursuit, regardless of the outcome. We admire the courage and determination of artists that are willing to endure struggle and hardship, but the only reason we know their stories is that these are the ones who have "made it," who have gained acclaim and financial success. What about the ones who devote themselves to their art without any recognition? There are plenty of actors, writers, and musicians that never get discovered but that continue to pursue their art nonetheless. These individuals serve as a cautionary tale—the kind that parents and teachers share with young would-be artists to save them, presumably, from a terrible mistake. After all, what seems more tragic or pitiful than the life of a failed artist?

Campbell maintained that the person who never even tries is far more tragic. In life, there are errors of commission and omission. Missed opportunities seem to inspire much more regret than failed ones. In describing the title character of his whimsical song, "The Man Who Couldn't Cry," Loudon Wainwright III wrote, "His novel was refused, his movie was panned, and his big Broadway show was a flop."[113] We find this character comical rather than tragic because at least he gave it his best shot!

"Because I have called, and you refused," reads the Book of Proverbs, "I also will laugh at your calamity; I will mock when your fear comes; when your fear comes as desolation, and your destruction comes as a whirlwind; when distress and anguish come upon you…For the turning away of the simple shall slay them, and the prosperity of fools shall destroy them."[114]

To miss out on the opportunity to embark on our creative adventure—the life path that is most likely to lead to the fulfillment of our potential and our destiny—may be the greatest tragedy that can befall any of us. Yet, this outcome is completely self-imposed. When Jesus said, "Many are called but few are chosen,"[115] he was referring to a process of self-selection. After all, who is keeping us from being chosen, other than ourselves? Our creative adventure awaits us, and the only obstacle in our way is our own willingness to say, "Yes!"

Do we get only one chance to jump onto our creative path? If we miss the boat, does it sail off permanently without us? There is no reason to think that the Call to Adventure is a one-time occurrence. Each of us may come across multiple windows of opportunity in the course of our lives. If we fail to open one, that is not necessarily a fatal error. But if we walk past enough of them without acting, eventually those windows turn into walls.

I have often wondered if the Call to Adventure might not be a daily occurrence. Every morning, we wake up to a blank slate. The day that awaits us can be virtually anything we make of it. We can begin the day by asking ourselves: *What will today look like? How can I make the most of this day?* The answer to these questions might be the very thing that propels us on our creative adventure. All it takes is one day or even one moment to launch us on our way. As Lao Tzu observed, "A journey of a thousand miles begins with a single step."[116]

In a fractal universe, one thing is clear: Each Call to Adventure represents multiple layers of opportunity. Our creative path consists of many adventures rolled into one. When we say "Yes!" to our creative adventure, we actually enter through the first of countless gates. In the life of an artist, a new Call to Adventure may materialize at every turn. After all, this call is nothing more than a catalyst—a set of circumstances that arouses our passions to the point of action. In theory, virtually anything can serve as that catalyst: the people we meet; the sights, sounds, and smells surrounding us; chance encounters; or the beauty we experience as we move through our daily lives. Every moment can be a Call to Adventure. By walking through one doorway, we discover an infinite number of others awaiting us. Each one represents an invitation to the dance, the adventure, the path of creative fulfillment.

The creative process always starts with a Call to Adventure. Something has to draw us into the creation cycle. If our passions are aroused, we can immerse ourselves completely in this cycle. But something has to arouse those passions. The right conditions must be in place. In many ways, those conditions depend on the decisions we have already made in our lives. Once we answer a Call to Adventure, we open ourselves to other opportunities. Inspiration begets inspiration. In the right frame of mind, the conditions are always in place for us to be inspired.

## Intuition

Based on his life experience, Joseph Campbell came to the following conclusion: "If you do follow your bliss, you put yourself on a kind of track that has been there all the while, waiting for you, and the life that you ought to be living is the one you are living. When you can see that, you begin to meet people who are in the field of your bliss, and they open doors for you."[117]

Once we have thrown ourselves into this creative adventure, the pieces seem to fall into place for us to move forward. As Campbell points out, we attract those mentors or guides that are willing and able to open doors for us. Sometimes, the guidance comes from another person—someone who is more experienced and has a broader perspective than we do. But more often than not, this guidance comes from an internal source, through a mechanism we call *intuition*.

In many ways, intuition is shrouded in mystery. It can be defined as something you know without knowing *how* you know. For knowledge to be intuitive, it has to come to us through a route other than our five senses or our thought processes. If we exclude these normal channels, what is left? How can we know something intuitively when we are unable to draw upon basic abilities like perception, memory, language, or inference?

Whatever intuition may be, we recognize it as an integral part of the creative process. For centuries, artists and visionaries have been making that much clear to us. "The really valuable thing is intuition," claimed Albert Einstein. "There comes a leap in consciousness, call it intuition or what you will, and the solutions come to you, and you don't know how or why."[118]

"Intuition is the essence of creativity," says filmmaker Ingmar Bergman. "I make all my decisions on intuition. I throw a spear into the darkness. That is intuition. Then I must send an army into the darkness to find the spear. That is intellect."[119]

I began studying intuition at a time when the field of psychology considered it to be nothing more than unconscious thinking. Even this narrow perspective was considered daring. Most researchers were unwilling to even acknowledge the existence of intuition. My Intuition in Pregnancy study may have helped change things by dispelling misconceptions and opening up new ways of looking at intuition.

In that study, my team interviewed hundreds of pregnant women receiving prenatal care services at a local women's health center. We asked these women to predict the sex of their unborn babies. Of the research participants whose predictions were based on an intuition (such as a dream or "gut feeling"), nearly 70 percent predicted correctly. Given that the chance of a lucky guess is roughly 50-50, this is quite a remarkable number. It suggests that women's intuitions about the sex of their child can be quite accurate, as long as they do not have an overriding preference for a girl or a boy. Those women who did show a strong preference were no better than chance at predicting the sex of their babies.

In the past two decades, the Intuition in Pregnancy study has drawn considerable attention, having been featured in *USA Today*, *Pregnancy* magazine, and NBC's *Today* show. What makes this study so compelling is that it captures a form of intuition that cannot be dismissed or explained easily. Clearly, a woman's intuition about the sex of her baby is not simply a form of unconscious reasoning. There is no known logic or inference that would allow a woman to arrive at such a conclusion. We also cannot make the case that a woman is using her perceptual abilities to make her prediction, because there does not seem to be any pertinent information that can be acquired through the five senses. If there were, we would expect more women to know the sex of their unborn child, and we might even be able to train people—or dogs, for that matter—to make correct predictions.

Something else is going on here. For nine months, mother and child share the same body. This intimate connection establishes a type of *intersubjectivity* in which the awareness and experience of the two become linked. So, how exactly does a mother know the sex of her baby? The answer is simple: She knows because at some level, she and her baby are one.

After more than a quarter-century spent studying and contemplating intuition, I have arrived at this conclusion: *When it comes to intuition, being is knowing.* A mother gains knowledge concerning her child because of the profound level of connection she feels with that child. At certain moments, she can experience a degree of closeness with her baby that extends beyond thought and certainly beyond words. She knows the physical and emotional needs of that baby as well as her own. A mother's empathy for her child is so complete that she often knows exactly what that child is feeling.

One of the basic tenets of Deep Creativity is that all creating is becoming. We know that the act of creating transforms consciousness into the universal mind, which encompasses all thoughts and all things. Intuition gives us a momentary glimpse into the limitless nature of that mind. For an instant, our perspective is expanded so that we take in much more than would be available to us normally. At such moments, the wisdom of the universe is at our fingertips— at least enough of it to gain new levels of awareness.

Whatever we aspire to create is already present within the universal mind. Through the power of intuition, we gain clarity beyond our normal understanding. This clarity is fleeting, especially when we are just setting out on our creative adventure. The beauty of intuition is that it gives us foresight when we need it most. Although we have not yet arrived at a point where we can adopt the perspective of the universal mind in a stable and lasting manner, we can catch enough of a glimmer to allow that perspective to guide us.

The universal mind contains the perspective of every wise teacher and brilliant artist that has ever lived. There is an idea, found in the Tibetan Buddhist practice of guru yoga, that each of us carries with us an inner teacher who is perfectly wise, fully awakened, and completely expansive. Although this inner teacher represents our true nature, explains Sogyal Rinpoche, "it has been obscured from beginningless time by a dark cloud of ignorance and confusion. This true nature, however…has never completely surrendered to the tyranny of ignorance; somewhere it is always rebelling against its domination."[120]

According to Rinpoche, our wise inner teacher is constantly working "to bring us back to the radiance and spaciousness of our true being."[121] Only the limitations of our own minds keep us from receiving the wisdom this inner teacher has to offer. But with the faculty of intuition at our disposal, the light of wisdom shines through the deepest darkness of our own ignorance. In the words of songwriter Harry Chapin, "There's a wild man wizard hiding in me, illuminating my mind."[122] That is intuition.

## Inspiration

Both the hero's adventure and the creative process are driven by the need to unlock and release the flow of life force. For the artist, this force is called creative energy, and it is the vehicle by which new ideas and outcomes are created. The artist releases this energy by tapping into the source of his or her inspiration.

The term *inspire* refers to the drawing in of breath. For millennia, energy has been linked to the breath. This is evident in the Sanskrit *prana* and the Hebrew *ruach*, which refer to both. Like the breath, creative energy is a precious gift. Both come from a mysterious source and grace our lives with their presence without actually belonging to us. We cannot hold onto creative energy any more than we can hold our breath indefinitely. Both forces are dynamic and can only sustain us if we allow them to keep moving. And the presence of both makes an unmistakable difference. Without breath, the body fails to thrive; without creative energy, the mind does.

Inspiration can be defined in a number of ways; with respect to creativity, it refers to the stimulus to do or feel something creative. When we are inspired, our creative juices flow in ways that get captured in our thoughts, experiences, and actions. Most of us would have no problem distinguishing works that are inspired from ones that are not, whether these works take the form of music, writing, art, movement, or poetry. Just as air breathes life into our bodies, inspiration breathes life into our creative endeavors.

In moments of inspiration, each of us taps into an unobstructed flow of creative energy and channels it towards specific outcomes. But when we are uninspired, it feels as if a giant dam is blocking that flow. Why is inspiration so unpredictable? We know that there is no switch we can flip or valve we can open to activate the flow of creative energy. The reason is that this energy is a gift, not a commodity. It does not belong to us and is therefore not under our intentional control.

Gifts come in and out of our lives unexpectedly and beyond our control. By their very nature, they are spontaneous and surprising. When we know that a gift is coming, some of its "giftness" seems to get lost. And although we Americans are not accustomed to the idea, gifts we receive must be given away again. One way or another, the gift has to keep moving. It is a force of nature that we cannot and must not contain.

A true gift is not something we can keep for ourselves. We cannot say for certain when a gift will come into our lives or when it will go. This being the case, we must always remain open to either possibility. The nature of a gift demands that it be received freely and given freely.

Creative energy is as much of a gift as anything in our lives. As you will recall, this energy takes two basic forms: love and joy. Love leads all of creation back to the Creator. In love, thoughts and things merge into the unity of pure consciousness. Joy leads the Creator into the creation. Through joy, consciousness gives rise to the universal mind, with its myriad ideas, images, and insights.

To be inspired, we have to be open to give and receive love, to give and receive joy. This openness does not guarantee inspiration. Ultimately, love and joy must find their way to us on their own. As with other gifts, we cannot control or predict the flow of creative energy, but we know that we are most likely to experience that flow if we can remain open to it.

In the next chapter, we will look at specific ways to do that. Although inspiration is an aspect of the creative process that we cannot control, we can put the conditions in place that are most conducive to it. That is all we can do. Going back to the creative trinity, we see why our adventure has to begin with the activation of creative energy. If we set out to expand our minds in a way that will encompass all of creation, or to escape the confines of our individual minds altogether, the creative process becomes extremely daunting. In the course of this process, both events are likely to happen, but only if we prepare ourselves properly.

Of the creative trinity—Creator-creating-creation—we begin with the act of creating because our actions have the greatest impact on our creative adventure, especially at the outset. In the Departure phase, we can set the table by opening ourselves to the flow of creative energy. That much we can do. And once the table is set, an enormous feast may follow. We have little say regarding how this feast will proceed or when it will be served. That is the beauty of any adventure, including the creative process. A mighty force gets unleashed, and we get swept up in it. We have no idea where this adventure will lead us or how it will change us, but we can be certain that it will be exhilarating and transformative. The trick, of course, is to remain as open as possible to receiving every gift the adventure has to offer.

# CHAPTER 10

# Initiation

*"You are the universe in ecstatic motion."*
—Rumi

C ampbell describes the second phase of the hero's adventure as a process of moving beyond the limitations of the past and into the realm of the unknown: "Once having traversed the threshold, the hero moves in a dream landscape of curiously fluid, ambiguous forms."[123] There, the hero encounters a series of trials and tests. Campbell refers to this phase of the adventure as the Initiation stage because this is the point at which the hero is tested, facing challenges and overcoming obstacles in order to move to the next level. Initiation, according to Campbell, "is the process of dissolving, transcending, or transmuting the images of our past."[124] The trials encountered at this stage are "symbolic of those crises of realization by means of which consciousness becomes amplified."[125]

In the creative process, the Initiation phase corresponds to the set of transformations that make it possible to transcend the limitations of our individual minds. In doing so, we do not simply gain access to the source of all creativity; we actually *become* the pure consciousness of the Creator. This transformation does not come easily. We have to surrender all of the mental constructs that define us, including our beliefs, judgments, memories, expectations, and concepts.

"The agony of breaking through personal limitations is the agony of spiritual growth," writes Campbell. "Art, literature, myth and cult, philosophy and ascetic disciplines are instruments to help the individual past his limiting horizons into spheres of ever-expanding realization."[126] The trials faced by the hero represent a stripping away of the past so that something new can emerge. In some cases, the hero must undergo death in order to be reborn.

In the Initiation phase, Campbell observes, the hero enters "a forgotten dimension of the world we know. And the exploration of that dimension, either willingly or unwillingly, is the whole sense of the deed of the hero."[127] The adventure leads the hero to an encounter with the goddess or mother, atonement with the father, and the attainment of what Campbell calls the "ultimate boon."[128]

Each of these milestones corresponds to a specific aspect of the creative process. Like the hero, the artist ventures into a mysterious realm, seeking to tap into the ultimate source of all creativity. Although this source is within anyone's grasp, few people choose to explore it. For the artist, the boon to be attained is not so much a creative product but rather the profound experience of inspiration that gives rise to such products. Here is a closer look at the key events that define the Initiation phase.

## Purification and Sacrifice

The hero's adventure is never easy. If it were, there would be nothing exceptional about it. But in actuality, it is an ordeal consisting of challenges that the hero must pass in order to advance. According to Campbell, the Initiation phase begins with a "road of trials."[129] These trials require the hero to sacrifice something of value. Each subsequent trial demands a greater degree of sacrifice.

The point of this sacrifice is purification. For the hero, the adventure is a quest for the ultimate boon, which is a taste of pure perfection. The boon can take many forms: on Mt. Olympus, gods and heroes feast on *ambrosia*; Japanese gods drink *sake*; in Persia, gods consume *haoma* distilled from the tree of life; for

Polynesians, this nectar is known as *ave*; and the Aztec gods drink the blood of pure-hearted men and women.

To attain the reward, the hero must prove worthy. The gates of paradise open only to those rare beings whose purity of spirit and intention have been tested and verified. In all cases, the test of purity involves letting go of the past. Only those who are willing to give up everything they cherish are considered worthy of the profound experience of transformation that the adventure can provide.

Campbell recounts a time when he took part in a powerful ritual held in a cave. The participants in the ritual were instructed to gather seven objects representing things that made life worth living for them. As they made their way through the cave, their passage was blocked by someone demanding that they surrender one of their objects, beginning with the least cherished. In order to leave the cave, each person had to give up all seven objects, and more importantly, the precious things that those objects signified.

Reflecting on this experience, Campbell noted its profound effect on the lives of the participants:

> I can tell you that the ritual worked. All of the participants with whom I talked had an actual experience of *moksa*, or release, when they had given up their last treasure. One damned fool was the exception. He did not give up anything. That's how seriously this ritual was taken. When he was asked to give up something, he just stooped down, picked up a pebble, and handed that over.[130]

To give up something we value deeply is far from easy. In the ritual Campbell described, one individual failed the test. In our daily lives, most of us fail. We hold on tightly to the people and things we cherish, and perhaps most tightly to ourselves. Imagine taking part in this ritual. What would be your most valued thing? For many of us, it would be our lives. To give up our lives would be the ultimate sacrifice—something most people would find impossible. And yet, in the end, that is exactly what each of us is forced to do.

In the road of trials, the hero must answer the following question: *Are you willing to lay down your life for this adventure?* The very question is what makes the adventure so heroic. Who among us would say "Yes"? Perhaps only the most reckless and foolhardy would agree to sacrifice their lives for something unknown. Yet, in actuality, we see it happening all around us every day. And whether we realize it or not, we may be making this type of sacrifice ourselves, without even realizing it.

No matter what we decide to do with our lives, we end up sacrificing our lives to something. We can choose to give our lives to our work, family, recreation, politics, adventure, or any number of other things. If we are unable to choose, then we hand over our lives to indecision.

Some choose to give their lives to a cause. "I only regret that I have but one life to give for my country," said American patriot Nathan Hale as he was about to be hanged by the British.[131] Others, like Jack London, give their lives to the spirit of adventure: "I would rather be ashes than dust; I would rather that my spark should burn out in a brilliant blaze than it should be stifled by dry-rot; I would rather be in a superb meteor, every atom of me in magnificent glow, than in a sleepy and permanent planet; the proper function of man is to live, not to exist."[132]

In the end, we all sacrifice our lives. The hero simply does it with full awareness and intention. Commonly, hero myths feature the theme of self-sacrifice. An excellent example of this is the prophet Jonah, who is commanded by God to go to a specific city and deliver a prophecy. Instead, Jonah tries to escape his fate by sailing in the opposite direction. The ship on which Jonah is sailing encounters a violent storm, and he instructs the sailors to throw him overboard in order to save themselves. This is his moment of self-sacrifice. As soon as the sailors cast him out, the sea calms, and Jonah is swallowed by a whale, where he spends three days and nights until God commands the whale to spew him out.

The belly of the whale, Campbell explains, represents self-annihilation. "The hero goes inward, to be born again."[133] The transformation that allows the hero to advance requires this level of sacrifice. None of the rewards of the adventure can be attained without it. Heavyweight prizefighter Joe Louis once remarked, "Everybody wants to go to heaven, but nobody wants to die to get there."[134]

Sacrifice and death always precede the ascension to heaven; there is simply no escape.

For the artist, sacrifice comes in the form of complete devotion to the creative pursuit. The French Romantic artist, Eugene Delacroix, wrote, "The practice of art demands the whole of a man; for him who is genuinely in love with it, devotion to the work is a duty."[135] Devotion to the creative life always comes before success, and that success is never guaranteed. The cliché of the starving artist has a basis in reality. Of the nearly 2000 paintings he created during his life, Vincent Van Gogh only sold one. He died penniless, as did a number of great artists, including William Blake, Franz Schubert, and Edgar Allan Poe. Although we admire the greatness of their work, we tend to overlook the degree of self-sacrifice they showed as they spent their entire lives in poverty and obscurity.

The self-sacrifice demanded by the creative process has both a macro and a micro component. At the macro level, we see that the decision to devote one's life to a creative pursuit comes at an extraordinary cost. The artist sacrifices stability and security for something greater. Just like the hero, the artist seeks the ultimate boon. But this reward is neither fame nor fortune; not only are such outcomes not guaranteed, they may be irrelevant altogether. It is the creative process itself, including the metamorphosis that the artist undergoes as a result of that process, which is most compelling. As a writer, I have no idea if anyone will ever read—much less care about—anything I have written. Yet, that is never my concern when I sit down to write. On my best writing days, I undergo a transformation that can only be described as magical. For a while, I disappear; time and space cease to exist, and my fingers just seem to find their way to the right keys without any effort on my part. How could I exert any effort, after all, when I am nowhere to be found?

This leads us to the micro component of self-sacrifice. Every time we set out to create something, we are faced with a series of decisions comparable to the hero's road of trials. One by one, we may have to give up some, if not all, of our most cherished assumptions and beliefs. Without this release, new ways of thinking may never emerge.

The term, "think outside the box," comes from research done with a classic puzzle known as the *nine-dot problem*.[136] The problem-solver is shown a grid of nine dots like the one shown here:

The classic nine-dot problem

The challenge is to connect all nine dots using only four straight, continuous lines that pass through each of the dots. In drawing these lines, the pencil must never be lifted from the paper. Most initial attempts to solve the puzzle fail because of an assumption imposed by the problem-solver but never implied in the wording of the puzzle. This assumption is that the lines must be confined to the boundaries of the grid. The only viable solutions involve lines that extend beyond the limits of the grid. In other words, to solve the puzzle, we have to "think outside the box." This means letting go of assumptions that prevent us from seeing new possibilities, including the actual solution.

The accepted solution to the nine-dot problem looks like this:

The four-line solution

There is even a solution that uses only three lines. This requires the realization that each of the nine dots has a certain diameter and occupies space. Why is that a particularly difficult leap to make? Those of us who took high-school geometry learned that a point occupies no space. Our tendency is to treat the nine dots as points, which they are not. These dots can and do occupy space. In fact, their size is not specified; we can make them any size we want. If they are large enough, we can connect them quite easily as follows:

The three-line solution

When it comes to the creative process, letting go of the old is a much greater challenge than discovering something new. In the nine-dot problem, our assumptions can get in the way, keeping us from finding the solution. Even our most inconsequential assumptions restrict our experience of the world in ways that prevent us from going deeper. Underlying everything we think and perceive is a hidden reality that can only be experienced through a process of purification. If each individual mind is a window into the world, we have to find a way to make that window as transparent as possible. Or better yet, we can shatter the glass and reach across the window to touch the profound truths on the other side.

The road of trials that the hero undergoes is a metaphor symbolizing the process by which the mind is cleared so that true insight can be gained. The trials are so arduous because the mind resists letting go. This is why small children do everything in their power to stay awake just a bit longer even when they are so exhausted that they are on the verge of collapse. It is also the reason that in guided group meditation, the instruction to relax and silence one's mind is usually accompanied by the sounds of coughing, throat-clearing, and other forms of restlessness.

Somewhere in our minds, the notion of surrendering our thoughts is equated with death. We have a self-preservation mechanism that keeps this from happening. It is called the *ego*. Each of us should be grateful for our ego, which prevents us from offing ourselves in a number of ways, including various forms of physical, social, and psychological death. Defense mechanisms implemented by the ego spare us from humiliation, alienation, incarceration, and other forms of self-annihilation. On a daily basis, the ego protects us from our own self-destructive impulses.

Ironically, the ego interprets our desire to clear our minds as one of these impulses. Creativity depends on a level of surrender that our own ego tends to view as self-destructive. The ego is reluctant to draw a distinction between self-transcendence and self-destruction. Yet, there is an important difference. Those of us engaged in self-transcendence understand that all death leads to rebirth. We realize that we are bound for heaven, and that there is only one way to get there.

Like the hero's adventure, the creative process is a self-transcendent act. We let go of everything we know, everything we hold dear, so that we can find our way, even momentarily, to the source of all creation. This act of surrender is purifying to an extent that most people will never comprehend. We are liberating ourselves of our *selves*, because the creative adventure we are undertaking demands that we travel light—so light that even one tiny little thought would weigh us down. Our self-concept is a more like a boulder strapped onto our backs. Before we can take flight on our adventure, we have no choice but to jettison this baggage.

## The Flow of Love

After undergoing and passing a series of tests, the hero encounters a female figure that, according to Campbell, "is the incarnation of the promise of perfection."[137] This paragon of femininity may take the form of a matriarch offering comfort and nurturance, a beautiful goddess, a sister with whom the hero reunites, or a bride whom the hero marries.

Campbell refers to this female figure as a *goddess*, describing her in the following way:

> She encompasses the encompassing, nourishes the nourishing, and is the life of everything that lives. She is also the death of everything that dies. The whole round of existence is accomplished within her sway, from birth, through adolescence, maturity, and senescence, to the grave. She is the womb and the tomb.[138]

The goddess symbolizes the flow of energy that fills and envelops all of creation. You will recall that creative energy comes in two forms: love and joy. In the merging phase of the creative process, it is love that dissolves the mind into pure consciousness. And what is the goddess, after all, but an embodiment of love? Whether it is the love of the mother for her child, or the love shared by woman and man, the entire "round of existence" is driven by this potent force that the goddess embodies.

Just as the hero struggles to break free of the past, the artist engaged in the creative process seeks liberation from the constraints imposed by the mind. The challenge facing the artist is to open up the mind just enough to allow the free flow of love. Each person's thoughts can act as a dam that blocks this flow. As we undo the powerful hold that our thoughts have over us, we begin to chisel away at the structure of the dam. First, tiny leaks start to develop, allowing love to trickle through in rivulets. Eventually, these streams grow larger, eroding the foundation of the dam until it bursts completely.

Most of us know what it is like to be immersed in love. Nothing else matters when we are consumed by its power. Falling in love is perhaps the most profoundly altered state of consciousness that many of us will ever experience. In writing about it, lyricists and poets have focused on certain qualities: spontaneity, suddenness, the element of surprise, and the loss of control. It has been compared to a rollercoaster ride, a drug-induced state, or falling off a building. There is a sense of complete surrender to a force that overpowers us with its intensity.

"The artist is the only lover," wrote dancer and choreographer Isadora Duncan. "He alone has the pure vision of beauty, and love is the vision of the soul when it is permitted to gaze upon immortal beauty."[139] For the artist, the creative process is all about love. How could it not be? Part of the reason to set out on this adventure in the first place is that it gives us a chance to do something we love. Artists talk about their art as if it were their lover, God, mother, father, best friend, and spouse all rolled into one.

Ralph Waldo Emerson once said, "Every artist was first an amateur,"[140] alluding to the origin of the word *amateur*, which comes from the French for "lover." The creative process itself bears a striking resemblance to falling in love. We want it, thrive on it, and welcome it, but at the same time we know we cannot control it in any way. There is no way to turn it on or off. We can only transform ourselves into a pure and open vessel to be filled by this love, if and when it does arrive.

So much of our society is built on this mystery of love. We would have no families without it. People would be less likely to come together to make babies—let alone, raise them. And we would not have the vast majority of things that human beings create. Most new technologies begin with the vision of one individual that loves the experience of imagining new things. We are all familiar with the story of Steve Jobs, whose innovations have impacted so many aspects of our lives, including the ways we use computers, listen to music, talk on the phone, take pictures, read books, and create our own art. "The only way to do good work is to love what you do," Jobs said.[141]

But it is not simply about loving what we do. The artist's love extends far beyond the creative process. French musician and composer Francois Delsarte conveyed this idea with incredible eloquence:

> If you own a telescope, what, may I ask, interests you in it? Why do you value it? Is it not because of the property it possesses of showing to your surprised eyes vast and profound perspectives, invisible without its aid? It is, then, the astounding views brought within range of your vision that you love the instrument for, and certainly you would not dare to say that you loved the telescope for the telescope. Now, art is the telescope of a supernatural world. In art, one must love something besides art if one would know how to love art.[142]

Having said all along that the emphasis of Deep Creativity is on the creative process, now I will veer in a different direction by making this declaration: *The process itself is not the ultimate reward of creativity.* We would like to think that the act of creating is its own reward. And there is little question about the rewarding nature of this creative adventure. Yet, there happens to be something more. In undertaking the adventure, we set out to attain something. Is that "something" the creative product? While not dismissing the value of what gets produced, I can assure you that the ultimate prize has little to do with the artifact remaining at the end of the creative process. Just as a trophy can be nothing more than a symbol of triumph, the creative product represents something much greater than itself, which can only be described as expansive and profound. Would you like to know what that is?

## The Ultimate Boon

A climactic moment in the hero myth takes place when the hero has an encounter with the father figure. This is no ordinary meeting. For one thing, it is often foreshadowed by a sense of dread. Facing the potential wrath of the father can be terrifying. Yet this figure also has a softer side. "In most mythologies," writes Campbell, "the images of mercy and grace are rendered as vividly as those of justice and wrath."[143]

The father possesses both of these aspects simultaneously. "In him are contained and from him proceed the contradictions, good and evil, death and life, pain and pleasure, boons and deprivations," Campbell explains. "He is the fountainhead of all the pairs of opposites."[144] This is because the father represents the Creator, whom we know to be the ultimate source and essence of all thoughts and all things.

Approaching the Creator can be a frightening proposition for a number of reasons. For one, it has to be preceded by a level of surrender that corresponds, in one way or another, to death. The ego interprets even the temporary silencing of the mind as a form of death—an interpretation that is actually quite accurate. In those silences, as in deep sleep, we cease to exist.

Perhaps even more terrifying, the Creator is the source and essence of everything—not just that which we find good or beautiful. The things we find most hateful and repulsive must also emanate from the same source. And often times, these paradoxical qualities co-exist in the natural world—not to mention our own human nature. Within us, we find elements of love and hate, kindness and brutality, nurturance and destructiveness. For every Gandhi, there is also a Hitler. The Creator abides equally in both, whether we like it or not.

According to Campbell, "The problem of the hero going to meet the father is to open his soul beyond terror to such a degree that he will be ripe to understand how the sickening and insane tragedies of this vast and ruthless cosmos are completely validated in the majesty of Being. The hero transcends life with its peculiar blind spot and for a moment rises to a glimpse of the source. He beholds the face of the father, understands—and the two are atoned."[145]

The Middle English origin of the word, *atone,* is: "at-one." Campbell refers to atonement in this sense, as a type of union between the hero and the father. Really, what happens to the hero at this point in the adventure is more of a *re*-union. The hero is returning to a primordial state, in which the father and the hero are one. The two would always remain in that state, except for the circumstances that pull them apart. Those circumstances are called: *life.*

Most mystical teachings include the idea that birth into a human embodiment leads to a sense of separation. We are living under the delusion that we are tiny, separate, and alone in this world, when we are actually part of the *web of creation,* so richly complex, multifaceted, and expansive that we cannot even begin to wrap our heads around it. These little minds of ours are most effective at splitting up the world into categories: us and them, black and white, good and evil. To experience "atonement with the Father," we have no choice but to move beyond those distinctions to the underlying unity.

When we immerse ourselves fully in the creative process, we have the opportunity to become one with the source of all creation. We return to our origin and essence, becoming wholly ourselves. This rebirth into wholeness may be the very reason we create in the first place, whether we know it or not. It appears to be among the most fundamental of human drives. As Abraham Maslow points out, "There is within the human being a pressure toward spontaneous expressiveness, toward full individuality and identity, toward seeing the truth rather than being blind, toward being creative, toward the good."[146]

To arrive at this point of wholeness, of perfect communion with the Creator, is to have triumphed. According to Campbell, "Those who know, not only that the Everlasting lies in them, but that what they, and all things, really are is the Everlasting, dwell in the groves of the wish fulfilling trees, drink the brew of immortality, and listen everywhere to the unheard music of eternal concord."[147]

The Creator is the wellspring of all joy. Recall that the universal mind emerges from consciousness in a burst of joy. This joy is spontaneous. It pours out of the Creator with the freedom and inevitability of a waterfall. Becoming one with the

Creator, we gain the fullest access imaginable to this powerful force of nature. Herein lies the reason why any one of us would undertake this creative adventure in the first place:

### Tenet #8: The ultimate reward of creativity is the sheer joy of the Creator.

The Buddha said, "When the mind is pure, joy follows like a shadow."[148] Purified of all thought, all struggle, and all division, the mind merges into the source of sheer joy. If you look closely at a waterfall, you will have no trouble seeing how dramatically it changes as it cascades. The joy that emanates from the Creator transforms the unity of consciousness into the multiplicity of the universal mind. Then, in a stream of love, this mind eventually returns back to pure consciousness. Love and joy come together to form bliss and ecstasy. These emotions propel the creation cycle ever onward. We experience the entire creation cycle as a cohesive whole by immersing ourselves completely in the Creator.

William Butler Yeats wrote, "All joyous or creative life is a re-birth as something not oneself, something which has no memory and is created in a moment and perpetually renewed."[149] The Initiation phase until this point has been a stripping away of the past—a type of death requiring complete surrender. All of this sacrifice results in rebirth and renewal, but not into the same type of existence that got left behind. Here and now, we are reborn into the *imperishable*, the very essence of all that is or ever will be. This imperishable essence has never been born and will never die. Yet it can be found within all mortal beings and every impermanent form.

Campbell describes it in the following terms: "This is the miraculous energy of the thunderbolts of Zeus, Yahweh, and the Supreme Buddha; the fertility of the rain of Viracocha; the virtue announced by the bell rung in the Mass at the consecration; and the light of the ultimate illumination of the saint and sage. Its guardians dare release it only to the duly proven."[150]

Remember: All creating is becoming. Through the creative process, we undergo a transformation that allows us to become one with the source of all creation. In actuality, we do not become the Creator. Rather, we strip away everything else within ourselves until the Creator is all that remains. The Creator has always been there, abiding in our hearts. There is only one consciousness permeating all of creation. We come to recognize that fact in the fullest and most intimate way possible when we let ourselves simply melt into it. Then, we serve as a wellspring from which sheer joy pours out into the world.

Through the process of Initiation, we prove ourselves worthy. This involves getting past the various obstructions preventing us from connecting with the source of our creativity and joy. All obstructions are self-imposed; we know that. The guardians that stand in our way are an army of mental constructs, including everything we have been taught about ourselves, about "reality," and about what is possible. Self-doubt acts as the ultimate barricade, forming a wall so high we can hardly see over it. But those of us who can get past all the roadblocks are rewarded with the ultimate boon, gaining access to a limitless source of joy.

This joy radiates steadily from the Creator, serving as the impetus for the emergence of the universal mind. Spontaneously and effortlessly, thought forms arise from consciousness. All thoughts are contained within the universal mind, which means that the moment we merge into the Creator, we gain direct access to every single thought that has ever existed. This access may be momentary. In a brief flash of insight, we attain perfect clarity. New ideas, images, and insights arrive in this way. If we could remain in this condition indefinitely, all the secrets of the universe would reveal themselves to us eventually. But most of us—even the most highly adept artists—only get an instant of revelation. Then we fall back into our individual minds. But how and when we do so makes all the difference, in terms of what we bring back from our creative adventure.

# CHAPTER 11

# Return

*"Only the artist comes and says: look inward, through what I have done, into your own starry heavens, yours alone."*
—Alexander Eliot

In the Return phase, the hero arrives home from the realm of the unknown, re-entering the mundane world that was left behind in the Departure phase. On the surface, the hero may appear to have ended up exactly where he or she started, but the circumstances associated with the Return are noticeably different from those at the beginning of the journey. For one thing, the hero who re-enters society is not the same person who ventured forth from it. Campbell writes, "The hero has died as a modern man; but as eternal man—perfected, unspecific, universal man—he has been reborn."[151] At this point in the journey, the hero's primary task, according to Campbell, "is to return then to us, transfigured, and teach the lesson he has learned of life renewed."[152]

Also, the hero brings back the reward or boon that has been gained through the process of Initiation. This treasure, which can take many forms (e.g., a sleeping princess, the Golden Fleece, or Holy Grail) serves as a "means for the regeneration of society as a whole."[153] Campbell maintains that "the great deed of the supreme hero is to come to the knowledge of unity in multiplicity and then to make it known."[154] By undertaking the journey towards realization, the hero becomes reborn and now has the resources with which to aid in the rebirth of an entire society. The discoveries that the hero shares with his or her society "are eloquent, not of the present, disintegrating society and psyche, but of the unquenched source through which society is reborn."[155]

Before these discoveries can be shared, the hero must cross what Campbell calls the *return threshold*. This is the boundary separating the mundane world the hero left behind from the "yonder zone" where the adventure unfolds and the ultimate boon is attained. At first, the hero may refuse to make this return, which makes perfect sense. Having witnessed the wonders of this other realm and experienced the highest levels of fulfillment there, the hero may have little inducement to come back to the ordinary, everyday world where most people spend their lives. Quoting the Upanishads, Campbell writes, "Who having cast off the world would desire to return again? He would only be *there*."[156]

Yet, the hero is compelled to return for a number of reasons. In some cases, the hero is "explicitly commissioned to return to the world with some elixir for the restoration of society," observes Campbell.[157] In others, the hero has obtained a particular trophy against the will of its guardian and must escape the wrath of gods, demons, or other entities. A chase may ensue, requiring the hero to adopt evasive tactics to avoid the obstructions placed in his or her path.

Sometimes, the world that the hero left behind has to come to the rescue. Campbell writes, "Society is jealous of those who remain away from it, and will come knocking at the door."[158] Even so, the society's acceptance of what the hero brings back from the adventure is not a given. In fact, the hero may be met by resistance and ridicule, placing him or her in the center of a battle that may not seem worthy of fighting, according to Campbell:

> The first problem of the returning hero is to accept as real,
> after an experience of the soul-satisfying vision of fulfillment,
> the passing joys and sorrows, banalities and noisy obscenities

of life. Why re-enter such a world? Why attempt to make plausible, or even interesting, to men and women consumed with passion, the experience of transcendental bliss? As dreams that were momentous by night may seem simply silly in the light of day, so the poet and the prophet can discover themselves playing the idiot before a jury of sober eyes. The easy thing is to commit the whole community to the devil and retire again into the heavenly rock dwelling, close the door, and make it fast.[159]

Yet, the hero is compelled by the work of "representing eternity in time, and perceiving in time eternity."[160] Eventually, the hero masters the ability to move freely between the two realms, coming to this profound realization: "The realm of the gods is a forgotten dimension of the world we know. And the exploration of that dimension, either willingly or unwillingly, is the whole sense of the deed of the hero."[161]

## Re-Entry

Astronauts know that the most challenging part of any space mission is the final stage. Having escaped the Earth's gravitational pull, they must then subject themselves to the trauma of re-entry. In the same way, most of us who escape the confines of our own minds in the course of our creative adventure will need to resume that mental activity at some point. The mind contains everything we know about ourselves and our world. To function as human beings, we need to have mental constructs—especially our self-concept.

The importance of the self-concept cannot be underestimated. Some psychologists have argued that we are only aware of anything to the extent that we can relate it to ourselves. Yet, our idea of who we are in relation to the world around us is constantly shifting. If we have the privilege to commune with the Creator of the universe, to tap into the source of sheer joy, and to gain the expansive perspective of the universal mind, we have no choice but to be transformed by the experience.

When we undertake our personal creative adventure, it changes us in important ways, expanding our horizons and giving us a glimpse of what is possible. Even if the adventure only lasts a fraction of a second, that could be enough to make the Return phase at least a little traumatic. In the words of Thomas Wolfe, "You can't go home again."[162] Immersed in the creative process, we might find ourselves in the same position as the genie in the bottle. Once released from that tiny prison, what would ever compel the genie to go back?

Of course, there are important reasons to re-assume the perspective of the individual mind, in spite of all its limitations. In our creative adventure, we gain at least momentary access to the universal mind. Every thought that has ever existed can be found there. Imagine walking into the richest library in the world, containing every great work of literature, art, music, poetry, and film. Unlike any other library, though, this one includes works that have yet to be discovered: books that have never been published, and paintings that have never been seen.

Our natural impulse is to share what we have witnessed. The only way to capture and convey these riches is through our thoughts, words, images, movements, and sounds. Everything we have done in the course of our lives has prepared us for this task. Now, our minds have to do the work of recording the wonders we have had the privilege to encounter.

In the course of our creative adventure, we have immersed ourselves in the creation cycle, which alternates between the essence of pure consciousness and the vastness of the universal mind. Of course, we want to stay in these expansive realms. Assuming we can, we still might not choose to do so. The reason is simple: Only through the activity of our individual minds can we begin to express the beauty and splendor of what we have experienced.

Here is the dilemma faced by the explorer: If you discover a remote paradise, do you keep it to yourself and just stay there, or do you come back to "civilization" in order to share your discovery? I believe we have a fundamental impulse as human beings to share the things that excite us, that bring us joy and delight, or that expand our horizons. Why else do we invest so much of ourselves into our creative pursuits? When we encounter something sweet and delicious, we naturally want others to taste it. The sweetness is only enhanced by sharing it with others—especially those that can appreciate it as much as we do.

# Recollection

Campbell likens the Return phase to awakening from sleep: "the passage of universal consciousness from the deep sleep zone of the unmanifest, through dreams, to the full day of waking."[163] In our dreams, the entirety of the universal mind opens up to us. For a few moments, we gain access to images and ideas far beyond the scope of our waking consciousness. The insights we glean from the experience depend on our capacity to grasp and recall them.

The depth or the breadth of what we can grasp depends on our mental abilities. It is not so much an issue of intelligence as of preparation. If you have never thought about particle physics, you may have trouble interpreting a dream image involving the collision of subatomic particles. Even if such an image were to occur, it is unlikely to see the light of day. After all, how are you supposed to recall something that makes no sense to you?

In the 1930s, psychologist Frederick Bartlett conducted a memory study in which a group of British college students heard a Native American folktale entitled "War of the Ghosts."[164] When asked to recall the story two weeks later, these students tended to omit or change certain elements, particularly those that were least familiar to them or inconsistent with their frame of reference. For instance, characters that were ghosts in the original story were transformed into living people in the version recounted by many of the students.

Even when we have a coherent dream that makes sense, we may still have trouble recalling it. Something seems to get lost in translation as we transition from sleep to waking. This can lead to forgetting and memory distortion, which only get worse the longer we wait to recall our dream images. Every second counts when we are trying to recollect something we have dreamt.

For instance, Samuel Taylor Coleridge claimed that he wrote one of his most famous poems, *Kubla Khan*, after taking opium that had been prescribed for pain and then falling asleep in his chair. Coleridge maintained that he composed more than two hundred lines of verse over the next three hours, all while he slept. In his journal, he wrote about the experience, referring to himself in the third-person: "On awakening, he appeared to himself to have a distinct recollection of the whole, and taking his pen, ink, and paper, instantly and eagerly wrote down the lines that are here preserved."[165]

Then, his writing was interrupted by a knock at the door. A person from a nearby town had stopped by to discuss a business matter. The meeting lasted about an hour, after which Coleridge returned to the task of writing down what he could remember of his dream. Much to his consternation, he discovered that "though he still retained some vague and dim recollection of the general purport of the vision, yet, with the exception of some eight or ten scattered lines and images, all the rest had passed away like the images on a surface of a stream into which a stone had been cast."[166]

The issue of recollection becomes particularly important during the Return phase. In a moment of clarity, we may have powerful realizations, make significant discoveries, or imagine ground-breaking new creations. By tapping into the universal mind, we gain temporary access to a vast reservoir of ideas, images, and insights. Although the individual mind may not have the capacity to conceive of these things on its own, it does have the ability—and perhaps even the responsibility—to grasp and recall them.

Recollection is like attaching a handle to something slippery and cumbersome. Have you ever tried moving a futon? Even though it is not all that heavy, the fact that a futon is so oddly shaped and provides no suitable hand-holds makes it particularly challenging to lift or maneuver. If you can tie a rope around it, suddenly you have something to hold onto, making it easier to carry.

Similarly, recollection of insights gained in the creative process can be simplified if we have a framework that allows us to think about and even discuss our ideas. We are attaching a handle of sorts to an experience that may be ineffable. Imagine entering the realm of the Creator, which is pure consciousness free of all thought and language. Suddenly, you gain access to the universal mind. Now, every thought that has ever existed is at your disposal. How can you take in everything? The answer, of course, is that you cannot. The only thoughts you can bring back from your inner journey are the ones you are able to recollect. You need handles that will permit you to grasp those thoughts and refer to them at a later time. If you can tell a story, paint a picture, or sing a song, for example, you can capture the insights gained from your creative experience.

Although the Return phase may be likened to awakening from a dream, sleep is not necessarily involved. The entire creative process can unfold while you are driving a car, taking a shower, standing in line at the store, drinking a beverage, walking in nature, or sitting in your favorite chair. It can all happen in an instant, reminiscent of the space travel in Carl Sagan's novel, *Contact.* The main character, Ellie Arroway, is propelled through wormholes to the center of the Milky Way—a journey that feels like hours to her but that takes mere seconds from the perspective of observers on Earth.[167]

In that briefest of instants, a life-changing experience can take shape. Campbell refers to the culmination of the adventure as *apotheosis*, a Greek term meaning, literally, "to make divine." This is the profound realization that the Creator is an indwelling presence within us. The objective of the Return phase, then, is not simply to recall words and images that can yield new creative products. I use the term *recollection* here because it has a second connotation that extends far beyond the simple act of remembering. It can also mean the attainment of a tranquil state through spiritual contemplation. Far more significant than any words or images, the person who has experienced apotheosis may seek to capture the *essence* of the experience so that others may share in it. And is that not the point of great art?

The recollection of the artist makes it possible for something transcendent to be conveyed through one's art. Interacting with that art, we find that it touches us to our core, helping us connect with the fundamental truths of human existence. Regardless of how many times these truths are conveyed, the message is always needed. We human beings can have a hard time remembering who and what we are. That is why artists and mystics are so invaluable. They offer us a chance to recollect something important that has been dissipated, ignored, or forgotten.

To help an entire society in the process of recollection is no easy task. Campbell points out the daunting nature of this challenge:

> How teach again...what has been taught correctly and incorrectly learned a thousand times, throughout the millennia, of mankind's prudent folly? That is the hero's ultimate difficult task. How render back into light-world language the speech-defying pronouncements of the dark? How represent on a two-dimensional surface a three-dimensional form, or in a

three-dimensional image a multi-dimensional meaning? How translate into terms of 'yes' and 'no' revelations that shatter into meaninglessness every attempt to define the pairs of opposites? How communicate to people who insist on the exclusive evidence of their senses the message of the all-generating void?[168]

In the creative process, the artist touches a core reality that is infinite and eternal—a mystery that stretches far beyond the capacity of the mind to comprehend. It is simply too vast to fit into our narrow way of thinking, too profound for us to fathom, and too close to be recognized. So, how exactly does one capture it?

In addressing this issue, German painter Max Beckmann noted, "My aim is always to get hold of the magic of reality and to transfer this reality into painting—to make the invisible visible through reality. It may sound paradoxical, but it is, in fact, reality which forms the mystery of our existence. One of my problems is to find the Self, which has only one form and is immortal—to find it in animals and men, in the heaven and in the hell which together form the world in which we live."[169]

Imagine trying to capture the invisible in images and the ineffable in words. This is the challenge that the artist has to confront. Much of the world's great, enduring art demonstrates the deftness with which the experience of the infinite can be caught by the artist working within the constraints of a specific medium or art form. The most masterful artists understand that the entire value of a creative product lies in its ability to convey this experience. "The creations which man makes manifest have no validity in themselves," wrote Henry Miller. "They serve to awaken, that is all."[170]

## Resistance

In the Return phase, the hero may encounter resistance, both from the guardians of whatever trophy or elixir the hero seeks to bring back to his or her society, and from society itself, which may fail to grasp or appreciate the significance of what the hero has done. These sources of conflict align with the kinds of issues that virtually every artist has encountered. There are essentially two forms of resistance that can pose threats to the culmination of the creative adventure.

## Internal Resistance

This stems from artists' reluctance or inability to share the profound experiences they have had. There are various forms of internal resistance. First is what Campbell describes as the "danger that the bliss of this experience may annihilate all recollection of, interest in, or hope for, the sorrows of the world."[171] Having experienced communion with the Creator—including the transcendent purity of consciousness and the vastness of the universal mind—any of us might be tempted to stop there. If you have been to the mountaintop, is that not enough? Why come down from those lofty heights? Having taken in the big picture, the artist or mystic may find the ordinary struggles of the everyday world to be alien or pointless.

Then there is the challenge of how to convey the experience of perfection. According to Campbell, "the problem of making known the way of illumination to people wrapped in economic problems may seem too great to solve."[172] An artist or mystic who has had a profound experience may feel little motivation to share it with those who are unlikely to grasp it. The experience itself may not translate; couching it in language that can be comprehended by someone who has never been there could seem like an insurmountable task. Not just anyone can capture something so delicate without crushing its essence. The true mastery of the artist lies in the ability to hint at transcendence with a brush stroke or a turn of phrase.

Virtually every artist has known self-doubt, regardless of age or experience. In his autobiography, *An Artist in America*, painter Thomas Hart Benton wrote, "When you've painted for years and discovered finally that you never get any nearer to a real mastery over your trade, a lot of very doubtful moments come on. Such moments increase with the years, and, no matter what your success, they keep occurring."[173]

Any number of doubts and questions may creep into an artist's mind: Is this a worthwhile pursuit? Am I up to the task? Am I doing justice to the subject? Does the work say what needs to be said? Could I have done it better? What if nobody else "gets" it? Even the most successful artists are susceptible to these types of doubts. When trying to capture something so profound in words and images, the enormity of the task can become overwhelming and cause virtually anyone to question their abilities and worthiness.

## External Resistance

This comes from a society that cannot comprehend the significance of the artist's vision. In some cases, Campbell observes, the artist "may meet with such a blank misunderstanding and disregard from those whom he has come to help that his career will collapse."[174] We often hear of visionary artists whose ideas have been met with rejection, indifference, and even scorn. The tales of society's resistance are all too familiar: Socrates being sentenced to death for his teachings; the trial of Galileo by the Inquisition for his heliocentric theory; the rejection of Margaret Mitchell's *Gone with the Wind* by virtually every major publishing house; and the public ridicule of Thomas Edison for his attempts to invent the light bulb.

"First they ignore you. Then they laugh at you. Then they fight you. Then you win." Whether or not Mahatma Gandhi actually said these words, which are often attributed to him, they capture perfectly the nature of external resistance.[175] Suppose you have had a realization of something that is both profound and subtle. You have had a glimpse of a core truth that resides far beyond the range of most people's everyday experience. The problem with trying to convey this truth is that the audience may be very limited. Those who have had a similar realization already understand, without your efforts, and those who have not, may never get it. When something is so far removed from the cultural mainstream, it may not even make enough sense to engage most people's attention. After all, how can they be expected to wrap their heads around something that they have never known first-hand and possibly never will?

If the message you are offering does manage to draw attention, chances are that the attention will be negative—in the beginning, at least. Your message may be subject to misinterpretation and ridicule because it has no basis in reality for most people. Modern mystics, for instance, run the constant risk of having their ideas dismissed as "non-scientific," which is a great stigma in an age when science is the pre-eminent worldview. And in fact, the label is quite accurate. Science depends on reproducibility, and nothing is more difficult to reproduce than a transcendent realization arising from a moment of inspiration. Regardless of the content of that realization, the epiphany that gives rise to it is inherently non-reproducible and therefore non-scientific. If the experience of the artist or mystic were perfectly reproducible, then there would be nothing particularly remarkable about it. To follow in the footsteps of these individuals requires a level of commitment and sacrifice that most people will never be able to achieve. That is why the creative adventure is so *heroic*.

Now, imagine that your realization or breakthrough gets enough people's attention that it has to be taken seriously. What then? If your message is about the unlimited nature of human beings, you may get recognized as a danger or threat to the status quo. The institutions that command authority do not want to see ordinary people become empowered. That is why so many great mystics throughout history have been persecuted and put to death. The Romans executed Jesus, whose primary message was one of unconditional love. Sufi masters such as Mansur al-Hallaj were tortured and burned at the stake. Just before he was doused with oil and set on fire, al-Hallaj declared: "All that matters for the ecstatic is that the Unique should reduce him to Unity."[176] And for centuries, the Roman Catholic Church ordered crusades against the mystical practice of Gnosticism, resulting in the imprisonment and death of entire groups, as well as the destruction of some of the most important Gnostic texts ever written.

Yet, the message of unity always prevails, in the long run. Much of the world's great art conveys it. We are surrounded by music, literature, architecture, and myriad other art forms that imbue our lives and our minds with this message. In spite of all attempts to dismiss, ridicule, or resist it, the message can never be suppressed. In the words of the Baha'i prophet, Baha'u'llah, "So powerful is the light of unity that it can illuminate the whole world."[177]

## Master of the Two Worlds

In the Return phase, the creative adventure reaches its culmination. As a result of this adventure, we realize that we have "been blessed with a vision transcending the scope of normal human destiny, and amounting to a glimpse of the essential nature of the cosmos," according to Campbell.[178] Although the entire adventure may unfold in a fraction of a second, its impact on our lives can be enduring. By delving fully into the creation cycle, we effect a reconciliation of our individual mind with something far more universal.

Having undergone this adventure, we gain what Campbell calls the "freedom to pass back and forth across the world division, from the perspective of the apparitions of time to that of the causal deep and back."[179] On a daily basis, we continue to live in the realm of form—of thoughts and things—limited by the constraints of space and time. But we also come to know something more essential: the purity of consciousness; the mediating power of love, joy, bliss, and ecstasy; and the expansiveness of the universal mind.

So, how do we reconcile these very different realms? Once we have gotten a taste of infinity, the task of returning to a finite existence may seem daunting. In the words of a popular World War I era song, "How ya gonna keep 'em down on the farm after they've seen Paree?"[180] The answer, of course, is that there is no going back. Once you have been granted freedom, you will not go back willingly into your prison cell. And once you have finally learned to fly, nothing can keep you grounded.

In our creative adventure, we have known what it is like to experience the universe from the perspective of its Creator. The only way we can return to our original human form, with all its limitations and frailties, is if we are able to derive some benefit from doing so. But also, we go back with the awareness that there is something more to who we are and what we can do, know, and experience. It turns out that the benefit and the awareness are related. This life we are living is a great privilege, as long as we understand the nature of that privilege. When we undergo our creative adventure, it reminds us that this is all an elaborate game we are playing.

In Sanskrit, the term *lila* (pronounced LEE-lah) means "divine play." It refers to the process by which the pure consciousness of the Creator embeds itself in all form, including humanity. In the Hindu sacred texts, the Creator, known as *Brahman*, declares, "I shall be many. May I manifest myself numerously."[181] The entire universe is seen as the divine play of a Creator that seeks only to experience all the varied forms that existence can take. According to Hindu scholar Ram Shankar Misra, the act of creation has no other purpose:

> Brahman is full of all perfections. And to say that Brahman has some purpose in creating the world will mean that it wants to attain through the process of creation something which it has not. And that is impossible. Hence, there can be no purpose of Brahman in creating the world. The world is a mere spontaneous creation of Brahman. It is a *lila*, or sport, of Brahman. It is created out of Bliss, by Bliss, and for Bliss. *Lila* indicates a spontaneous sportive activity of Brahman as distinguished from a self-conscious volitional effort. The concept of *lila* signifies freedom as distinguished from necessity.[182]

In the end, all of our creative pursuits are an opportunity to identify with the Creator hidden within us. In so doing, we become active participants in the *lila* that is constantly unfolding throughout the universe. This divine play is happening regardless of what we choose to do. Even if we refuse the Call to Adventure, we are still taking part in it. But there is a big difference between being the creature or the Creator. The creature is like a chess piece that gets moved around by forces outside of its control, whereas the Creator is the one that moves all of the pieces on the board. If given a choice, which would you rather be?

In the *lila* that is being played out, here and now, the Creator does not simply move the pieces on the board but actually embeds itself in them. The Creator can assume any form without being confined to it. By the time we reach the Return phase of our creative adventure, we have discovered that we share in this ability. All of the capabilities we cultivate through this adventure make it possible for us to create by becoming.

In a famous poem, the 8th Century Indian philosopher Adi Shankara wrote:

> Sometimes a fool, sometimes a sage, sometimes possessed of regal splendor; sometimes wandering, sometimes as motionless

as a python, sometimes wearing a benign expression; sometimes honored, sometimes insulted, sometimes unknown—thus lives the man of realization, ever happy with supreme bliss. Just as an actor is always a man, whether he puts on the costume of his role or lays it aside, so is the perfect knower of the Imperishable always the Imperishable, and nothing else.[183]

Through our creative adventure, we learn to create by becoming. First, we merge into pure consciousness. Then we participate in the sheer joy through which form arises from formlessness. We discover that we can tap into the universal mind, which encompasses all things and all thoughts. And by the Return phase, we have managed to capture the most salient and precious ideas, images, and insights to bring back from our adventure so that we can share them with others.

Most importantly, we become one with the Creator abiding in us. We come to realize that the entire creation cycle is unfolding right here, right now, deep within us. Just like the hero, we set out to transform the world in some way, and we end up transforming ourselves. As long as our imagination remains active and our intuition clear, we can make ourselves into anything we wish, adopting any form, playing any role, or wearing any disguise. This is the ultimate creative power.

# CHAPTER 12

# The Deep Six

*"We are born with the power to alter what we are given at birth."*
—Anaïs Nin

**D**eep Creativity differs from every other approach to the study of creativity in two ways: 1) we emphasize the creative process; and 2) our methods involve a first-person approach. Everything you have learned about the creative process so far is based on the accounts of individuals like me that have experienced it first-hand. At some point, you may want to verify these startling discoveries for yourself, which means undertaking your own creative adventure. The future of Deep Creativity depends on intrepid explorers like you who are not only willing but eager to delve into the realm of mystery and gain precious insights into the core truths of human existence.

You may or may not have what it takes to immerse yourself in the creative process this deeply. In Deep Creativity, the prototypical explorer possesses six qualities, called the Deep Six, which are crucial for success. The good news is that these qualities are not genetic traits. Virtually anyone can develop and exhibit them. As with so many other talents and attributes—especially those related to creativity—the refinement of the six qualities we are about to discuss takes time and dedication. It is more a matter of personal choice than innate ability.

For decades, psychologists have engaged in the *person-situation debate.* At the heart of this controversy is a simple question: Does human behavior depend more on stable, long-term attributes of the person, or on the set of circumstances in which people find themselves? With respect to creativity, in particular, personality psychologists would argue that individual differences in creative behavior are a function of personality traits such as openness, intrinsic motivation, self-confidence, and intelligence, which are presumed to remain consistent over time and across situations. Opponents of the trait approach, who call themselves *situationists,* would argue that people are not consistent enough over time to be characterized by broad personality traits. Creativity, then, would be more dependent on the set of conditions in which the individual is placed than on stable personality traits. Given the right conditions, virtually anyone can display creative behavior.

In actuality, the correlations found between creativity and various personality traits are generally in the neighborhood of 0.4, which is fairly small. To put this in perspective, if you want to predict the variability in people's creativity scores based on a particular personality trait, you would multiply 0.4 by itself, to get a value of 0.16. This means you would only be able to account for 16% of the variability in people's creativity based on that trait. That is not very impressive. Intelligence, which is perhaps the most well-studied of all personality traits, has an unclear relationship to creativity. Many researchers have proposed a threshold hypothesis, which suggests that a person needs a minimal level of intelligence to be creative; beyond that threshold, intelligence is not especially predictive of creative behavior. One of the biggest problems with the threshold hypothesis is that researchers cannot seem to agree on where the threshold lies. It can range anywhere from slightly below-average to significantly above-average.

In important ways, situationists have won the debate. There is plenty of evidence that human behavior is not consistent across situations. We may act compassionately in some situations and cruelly in others, depending on the conditions we face and the ways in which our behavior gets rewarded. The situationist position is consistent with the Buddhist doctrine of *emptiness*, which maintains that nothing exists as an independent entity.

"Phenomena do exist," explains Lama Yeshe, the Tibetan Buddhist master. "It is their apparently concrete and independent manner of existence that is mistaken."[184] Consider something simple, like an MP3 player. It begins as an idea conceived by an individual and then turned into a detailed design by a group of engineers. The components are made from raw materials mined in various parts of the world. A factory in China assembles the device, packages and ships it to a distribution center from which a truck delivers it to a store near you. Once you buy it, you bring it home, load your favorite music onto it, and use it for a period of time, until you tire of it or it stops working. If you throw it in the garbage, it gets hauled by a truck to a landfill. There it gets buried in a mound of plastic bags filled with household trash, awaiting the next step in its continuous transformation. Perhaps the materials will break down eventually through exposure to heat, pressure, water, wind, and microbes. Or future scavengers may find ways to reuse or take advantage of the materials at a time when the Earth's resources have become depleted.

Regardless of what happens, the MP3 player does not have an independent existence. At various points in time, it goes from being an idea, a collection of minerals buried deep in the Earth, an integrated design, a set of components waiting to be assembled, a livelihood for a factory worker, a finished product, a package to be shipped, a commodity to be sold, a coveted treasure, a source of profit, a way of listening to music, a piece of garbage, a means of survival for scavengers, or perhaps the starting point for an entirely different product.

According to Lama Yeshe, "We see it as something that grew out of causes, that depends on many things for its existence, that functions this way and that; this understanding will soften the general impression we have that it is something independent and concrete, existing out there as a solid, self-contained object."[185] The same can be said of the self. Although we may think of ourselves as having a concrete, well-defined identity, we may have trouble finding this hypothetical self if we set out to really look for it. Instead, we may discover, in the words of Lama Yeshe, "that what we are is only the result of giving a name or label to a group of ever-changing mental and physical parts."[186]

To a large degree, we can choose the mental parts that define us. Creativity is not an elusive personality trait that only a select few have the good fortune to possess. If we develop the right qualities within ourselves, we will have what it takes to pursue our creative adventure. These qualities, known as the Deep Six, can be remembered using the simple mnemonic: **PQRSTUV**. This stands for:

**P**assion
**Q**uiescence
**R**eceptivity
**S**elf-**T**ranscendence
**U**nconventionality
**V**ision

Let's look at each of these qualities in more detail.

## Passion

As a society, we have a conflicted relationship with passion. On the one hand, we know that the kind of intense emotion associated with passion can be a driving force in our personal and professional lives. On the other hand, there is a sense that passion can be dangerous and destructive. The term itself comes from the Latin *pati*, meaning "to suffer" or "to endure." Passion was first associated with the suffering of Jesus and other martyrs. This type of suffering has always been a matter of choice. Devotion to something greater—perhaps a principle or ideal—lies at the heart of martyrdom.

Like martyrs, artists devote themselves to something greater. That devotion always requires sacrifice. It is the artists' passion that makes this type of sacrifice possible. Artists often give up comfort, security, and other benefits in favor of their creative pursuits. This requires a level of drive, enthusiasm, and excitement that most people lack. Strangely, the majority of people never discover where their passions lie. Artists have not only discovered their passion for the creative adventure; they have made that passion the highest priority in their lives.

The importance of passion to the creative process cannot be underestimated. Here is what a number of renowned artists have said about it:

Mere enthusiasm is the all in all... Passion and expression
are beauty itself.
—William Blake[187]

What one wants is unrestrained passion, fire for fire.
—Henry Miller[188]

Success comes to those who dedicate everything to their
passion in life.
—A. R. Rahman[189]

Nothing great in the world has been accomplished without
passion.
—George Hegel[190]

This I know, that nothing is so eloquent in due season as
real passion, for it seems to be the prophetic utterance of some
possessing spirit, and to inspire every word.
—Cassius Longinus[191]

Passion is the one great force that unleashes creativity,
because if you're passionate about something, then you're more
willing to take risks.
—Yo-Yo Ma[192]

Each of us has a number of gifts at our disposal, but passion is our *core* gift.
Like any gift, it comes from a mysterious source. We have no way of knowing
why we feel so passionately about specific people, places, activities, animals,
plants, or thoughts. We just do. And it seems that all of us have some value
or ideal that touches us in a way that nothing else can. It may be a passion for
learning, a love of beauty, a desire for competition, or a yearning for community.

Some people discover their core gift at an early age. For example, at age two, Wayne Gretzky would watch hockey games on TV with his parents, and when the games ended, he would cry disconsolately. The reason for his tears was that he did not want the games to end. According to Malcolm Gladwell, Gretzky's great gift as a hockey player is his passion—more so than his talent, skating ability, or vision: "This guy loves the game so much that he would do nothing but play it and think about it and engage it."[193] Gretzky himself agreed with this conclusion, noting that "maybe it wasn't the talent the Lord gave me—maybe it was the passion" that made him such an exceptional player.[194]

Others never find their core gift. When I have taught workshops on this topic, I have had people in their 70's approach me and say, "I still don't know what I want to be when I grow up." Although it is never too late to discover your driving passion in life, I do wonder why it takes so long for so many individuals to get there. My experience in these workshops is that when people identify their core gift, they are not surprised. Somewhere in the back of their minds, they already know it. But for some reason, they may be reluctant to acknowledge it fully. Why would that be?

I discontinued these workshops when I realized that the knowledge participants were gaining about their core gift often triggered fear and other forms of resistance. In my naiveté, I had thought that I was offering people something beautiful and profound—the chance to know an important part of themselves. For some of the workshop participants, this was exactly the case. But for others, the knowledge turned out to be more of a burden than a privilege. Once you find your passion for something, then you have to ask yourself: *What do I do with this knowledge?*

Having a strong passion and dedicating yourself to it are two different things. Just as some would-be heroes refuse the Call to Adventure because they are not up to the challenge, so it is that most of us prefer not to know the source of our greatest passion because we are not ready to devote our lives to it. Artists are heroic because they choose a life path that may very well be filled with hardship and challenges most people do not want or need to face. When you pursue your passion, you quickly sacrifice the safety net of social acceptability. Essentially, you have veered off a well-marked road and onto an overgrown path requiring some serious bushwhacking. Along that path, you are likely to encounter struggle, humiliation, and ridicule. Friends and family will let you know in no uncertain terms that your actions are misguided, irresponsible, or even insane.

But the benefits far outweigh the risk. Passion is the springboard to limitless fulfillment and creativity. When we throw ourselves into our passions fully—heart and soul—regardless of the consequences, doors invariably open for us. The pursuit of any one passion may lead to the discovery of many others. For instance, my passion for a woman I loved inspired me to follow her to Ecuador, where I had the chance to travel to the Galapagos Islands. There, I discovered my passion for coral reefs, which led me to the South Pacific three years later. When I was in Australia, I had a profound experience, described in Chapter 15. This experience was the inspiration for the ideas you are reading now.

I used to think that passion was a function of age. When I was a teenager, I was passionate about everything that interested me: music, environmental issues, basketball, films, and science. It seemed to me that most adults had either disregarded or lost track of their most intense passions. The grown-ups I encountered, for the most part, seemed lifeless and wooden. I wondered how it was possible to live a life so devoid of passion.

Then, when I started teaching at the college level, I found that my 18-22 year-old students were—for the most part—equally out of touch with their passion. When I would ask them to describe the things in life about which they were most passionate, I found the vast majority of their answers to be sterile. Granted, few students want to share such intimate information with their instructor, but it was not just that. Many of them confided to me, one-on-one, that they really had no idea where their passions lie.

So, it would seem that the issue is societal. Rarely does anyone ask us about the things that inspire passion in us. In school, we are not taught how to identify the sources of our passion. Our society seems to undervalue it, even though virtually any artist will tell you that it is one of the most important forces in their lives. The artist's passion is what draws us to their creations. The French impressionist painter Auguste Renoir said, "The work of art must seize upon you, wrap you up in itself and carry you away. It is the means by which the artist conveys his passion. It is the current he puts forth which sweeps you along in his passion."[195]

The entire creative process hinges on passion. It is why we answer the Call to Adventure in the first place, and why we leave behind the safe and familiar to explore the unknown. Without passion, it is hard to imagine that anyone would ever create beautiful works of poetry, art, literature, music, or architecture. This being the case, those of us interested in creative pursuits would want to know how we can cultivate passion within our own hearts.

The key is to know *and* embrace our passion. Those two steps must be inseparable. If we become aware of our passion but are unprepared to make it a priority in our lives, then it can become a destructive force. In the back of our minds, we will know that we chose to disregard a potentially limitless source of joy, fulfillment and inspiration simply because it was going to inconvenience us or make our lives harder. Living with this knowledge could be devastating. Imagine the regrets someone could take to their grave if they ended up choosing the "sensible" life path over the inspired one.

That is why I would caution anyone that wants to know their core gift: If you are not prepared to make it the focal point of your life, you are better off not knowing. But if you know in your heart that you are meant to pursue your creative adventure, then you will not be surprised to learn the nature of your core gift. There is a good chance you already know what it is.

Here is a simple exercise designed to bring you in contact with your core gift: Recall a time in your life when you were so happy, so filled with joy, that nothing else mattered. At that moment, you lost yourself completely in what you were doing or feeling. You felt absolutely no worries or cares. Everything seemed perfect and complete, and time stood still.

Once you have come up with that memory, let it become as vivid as possible. What details do you recall? When and where did it happen? What were the circumstances that gave rise to the experience? How did it unfold? And what feelings did it evoke in you? The more details you can recall, the better. Write down everything you can remember, including any impressions, thoughts, feelings, or sensations that come to mind.

The next step requires an element of intuition. You may need to be patient with it. When I used to lead workshops related to the core gift, I often assisted participants with this task: Identify the central element of the experience. What made it so profound and memorable for you? Give that element a name or label. This may take a while. You are better off just letting something come to you rather than forcing yourself to generate an answer.

I have helped hundreds of people identify and name their core gifts. Some names are simple: Beauty, Humor, Family. Others are more complex: the Music of the Moment; Inspired by Inspiration; the Competitive Edge. Giving your core gift a name makes it easier for you to think and talk about it. You turn it into something less abstract or esoteric. It becomes a tangible force in your life and will help you determine your overall direction if you let it. So, you might as well know what to call it.

When you are ready to throw yourself into your creative adventure, knowing your core gift can be extremely beneficial. It can help you focus, and it can also remind you on a daily basis of what it is that drives you. Every kind of success comes to those who can answer the simple question: *Why?* Many people are unable to generate a satisfactory answer. Often, their lives move in a particular direction based on circumstance and nothing more. But artists always know why they do what they do. They have made a conscious, intentional choice to devote themselves to a particular pursuit, and that choice can become the starting point for a life filled with creativity and delight.

## Quiescence

The reason that passion is so critical to success, not just for the artist but in virtually any field of endeavor, is that it breeds single-mindedness. If you are passionate about an activity, you can devote yourself to it for hours on end. Artists engaged in the creative process display a level of concentration that most people will never know. Concentration can serve as a catalyst for the psychological transformation that artists must undergo in order to tap into the source of their creativity.

Psychologists have established a link between creativity and an experience they call *absorption*, which is defined as the total commitment of attention to a single object. When individuals are absorbed in an activity, they may forget about everything else. If they are absorbed in a memory of the past or a fantasy of the future, they might experience such clarity and vividness that it would seem as if the imagined event were taking place at that very moment.

The capacity for absorption can be developed, which is why concentrative techniques are used in meditation. For instance, yoga offers a wide range of techniques requiring the individual to focus complete attention on a sound (*mantra*), visual image (*mandala*), hand gesture (*mudra*), physical posture (*asana*), breathing pattern (*pranayama*), or other object. As absorption increases, the mind undergoes an important transformation.

Normally, attention shifts continuously and rapidly from one thing to the next, without staying on any one object for very long. In Buddhism, this mode of attention is likened to a monkey in a tree, jumping endlessly from one limb to the next. If our *monkey mind* can hold still for even a few moments, something changes. As the mind stays focused on one thing for an extended period of time, it eventually goes silent.

The capacity to achieve mental silence, which is called *quiescence*, can be instrumental to the creative process. "Every great work," wrote Pope John Paul II, "is born in silence."[196] This is because the entire process unfolds in a realm beyond thought. Remember **Tenet #1: Creativity is not what you think**. At certain points in the creative process, thinking can actually be counterproductive. We seek to tap into pure consciousness, which exists devoid of all thought. The only way to do this is by silencing our minds completely.

Many members of our society, including several noted consciousness researchers, have argued that this task is not only difficult but impossible. According to this view, the mind will remain active for the duration of a person's life. "There is no such thing as an empty space or an empty time," claimed John Cage. "There is always something to see, something to hear. In fact, try as we may to make a silence, we cannot."[197]

Mental silence is considered impossible by those who have never experienced it. And we live in a time when silence has become increasingly difficult to achieve. More than half a century ago, abstract artist Hans Jean Arp predicted: "Soon silence will have passed into legend. Man has turned his back on silence. Day after day he invents machines and devices that increase noise and distract humanity from the essence of life, contemplation, meditation."[198]

The reason so many people doubt the existence of mental silence is that they have never encountered it for themselves. Virtually no aspect of modern life makes room for it. We fill our lives with mental activity. Even when we are "relaxing," we are probably staring at a device, holding a conversation, or occupying our minds in any number of ways. Some of us need to have the television on in order to fall asleep. We cannot or will not surrender our mental activity even for a few precious moments so that we can experience the perfect silence of deep sleep. It comes as no surprise, then, that 45 percent of Americans report that poor or insufficient sleep has affected their daily activities at least once in the past seven days.[199] As a society, we have forgotten how to rest, how to sleep, and how to silence our minds.

Those of us who have not only experienced mental silence but who actually cherish it have no doubt that it exists. To us, it even seems a little far-fetched that we have to defend its existence. Yet this is exactly what has to be done. So, consider what happens when one thought is complete and the next thought has not yet entered your mind. There has to be a space between thoughts. Even if it only lasts a fraction of a second, this space must exist. Thoughts come into our awareness sequentially. You can tell that from your own experience. Rarely, if ever, do you have the experience of attending to more than a single thought at any given time. One thought is succeeded by the next, and no matter how close together they occur in time, there has to be some sort of gap between them.

Quiescence is simply the ability to extend that gap—to open up the space between thoughts more and more. You might be tempted to assume that the absence of thought is an experience of nothingness, but this is not the case. In actuality, mental silence creates an opening in which we are able to align most fully with consciousness. The source and essence of all thoughts and all things abides consistently within us. Most of the time, it gets drowned out by the chatter of our minds. The beauty of mental silence is that it allows us to commune with the Creator, immerse ourselves in the creation cycle and engage fully in the playful dance that is creativity.

To develop your quiescence, try closing your eyes and taking slow deep breaths. Make sure you are in a comfortable position. Fill your lungs with air slowly and steadily, and then empty them in the same way. Once your lungs are empty, just rest in that emptiness for a moment before drawing in your next breath. There is a wonderful peace you can feel at that moment, if you allow yourself. When your lungs are empty, your mind can follow suit quite easily. Do not concern yourself with taking your next breath. That is going to happen with or without your conscious effort. Just relax into the experience of emptiness for as long as it lasts. This might be no more than a second or two, but it represents the start of something big. Once you have experienced even the briefest flash of mental silence, then your foot is in the door, metaphorically speaking. Now, you can just allow that door to open a little bit wider each time you try it. Eventually, you will not need to link the experience of mental silence to your breath. You will be able to breathe normally and let your mind silence itself just by making the intention to do so.

With quiescence comes receptivity. When you learn to maximize your openness to new experiences, everything changes. This is when you enter more fully into the realm of Deep Creativity.

## Receptivity

Perhaps no quality is more important to the creative process than receptivity. Ultimately, the source of all ideas, images, and insights can be found outside the limits of the individual mind. The artist's challenge is to remain open and receptive to this source. That is by no means a simple task. It requires shifting away from the mind's normal and overriding mode of operation.

Researchers who study human consciousness keep arriving at the same conclusion, which is that the conscious mind can operate in one of two ways. As far back as 1890, the grandfather of American psychology, William James, observed, "There are two ways of knowing things. Knowing them immediately or intuitively, and knowing them conceptually or representatively."[200]

If you are like most people, you spend your waking life in what is known as the *active mode* of consciousness, which is dominated by goals, expectations, and strategies. In this mode, the mind is occupied by a steady stream of thought. The focus of attention moves continuously and rapidly from one thought to the next—often for long periods of time without interruption.

As we have already discussed, each of us is also capable of having a conscious experience free of all thought. This immediate and intuitive way of knowing is the function of a second mode of consciousness, called the *receptive mode*. In the receptive mode, the stream of thought that characterizes the active mode does not seem to exist. This mode relies more on images and sensations than on logical thought. Attention in the receptive mode seeks to draw in everything at once rather than jumping from one thought to the next. The emphasis is on "intake of the environment rather than manipulation," says psychologist Arthur Deikman, who has written extensively about the bimodal nature of consciousness.[201] Deikman points out that receptivity should not be mistaken for passivity. "'Letting it' is an activity, but a different activity than 'making it'."[202]

With respect to creativity, psychologist Rollo May has a similar view: "The receptivity of the artist must never be confused with passivity. Receptivity is the artist's holding him or herself alive and open to hear what being may speak. Such receptivity requires a nimbleness, a fine-honed sensitivity in order to let one's self be the vehicle of whatever vision may emerge."[203]

Even the most conservative researchers would acknowledge the link between receptivity and creativity. One of the personality traits most consistently associated with creativity is *openness to experience,* which is part of the Five-Factor Model of human personality.[204] Openness as defined in this model consists of six dimensions: active imagination, aesthetic sensitivity, attentiveness to inner feelings, preference for variety, and intellectual curiosity. People who are high in openness are motivated to seek new experiences and engage in self-reflection. By its very nature, the construct of openness implies a capacity to engage with the world in a receptive manner. Rather than impose one's will on a situation, the open individual allows it to unfold, observing what is taking place rather than simply reacting to it or disregarding the situational cues altogether.

Artists and mystics have long realized the importance of openness and receptivity to their creative process:

> Openness, patience, receptivity, solitude is everything.
> —Rainer Maria Rilke[205]

Always be open to inspiration. You never know where it may come from. Begin with an open mind, end with an inspired heart.

—Sheri Fink[206]

It is not a pumping-in from the outside that gives wisdom; it is the power and extent of your inner receptivity that determines how much you can attain of true knowledge, and how rapidly.

—Paramahansa Yogananda[207]

How long will this last, this delicious feeling of being alive, of having penetrated the veil which hides beauty and the wonders of celestial vistas? It doesn't matter, as there can be nothing but gratitude for even a glimpse of what exists for those who can become open to it.

—Alexander Shulgin[208]

By surrendering, you create an energy field of receptivity for the solution to appear.

—Wayne Dyer[209]

Purity is receptivity, the ability to sit and wait patiently, for as long as necessary, for the coming of the light.

—Frederick Lenz[210]

Both the active and receptive modes of consciousness play an important role in the creative process. In the Introduction, I mentioned Wallas' four-stage model of the creative process: preparation, incubation, illumination, and verification.[211] Of these stages, the active mode is instrumental in the first, *preparation*, and the last, *verification*. Preparation is everything we do to get ourselves to the brink of creative illumination. This includes all of the decisions and plans we make along the way, from the biggest (life direction) to the smallest (how we use this precious moment). Each of these choices takes planning, strategizing, goal-setting, and problem-solving, which are the strengths of the active mode. Here, logical thinking is an asset, as it is in the verification stage, when we test our creative insights to see if they are grounded in truth and functionality.

But the active mode plays a lesser role in the other two stages: *incubation*, when new ideas are on the verge of being realized, and *illumination*, when full realization takes place. These two stages rely, in fact, on our ability to transition from the active to the receptive mode. We must immerse ourselves in the creation cycle in order to gain new insights, make profound breakthroughs, and come up with bold new discoveries. Although the content of these epiphanies may be new to our individual minds, it already exists within the universal mind. Our primary challenge is to access this content, which takes receptivity.

There is no need to be receptive to something if we already possess it. In the active mode, we are limited to the knowledge that is available to our individual minds. But in the receptive mode, we break free of the confines of our own minds to merge into pure consciousness. Now, we are drawn into the creation cycle, when the universal mind, with all its thoughts and possibilities, can emerge from consciousness. For at least a moment, we have an infinitely vast knowledge base at our disposal. Our awareness expands to encompass all of creation. And this entire process unfolds as a result of our own receptivity.

Mindfulness meditation techniques are designed to enhance our receptivity. These techniques allow the practitioner to take in as much as possible of the present moment without judging, struggling, or grasping. "Only this actual moment is life," writes Thich Nhat Hanh. "Mindfulness helps you go home to the present."[212] A simple way to attain this homecoming is by being fully receptive to the conditions in which we find ourselves at this moment. "We have more possibilities available to us in each moment than we realize," he adds.[213] The key, of course, is to remain open to those possibilities.

People who try mastering mindfulness meditation often find it challenging. Learning how to retrain the mind is not necessarily easy. This is why I developed a very simple alternative, along with health psychologist Jhan Kold. This alternative, called Repose, involves lying on one's back on a flat comfortable surface with arms extended perpendicular to one's torso, palms up, legs open, and jaw relaxed, as show here[214]:

Repose

We have found that spending seven minutes in Repose three times a day (morning, afternoon, and evening) has a number of physical and mental health benefits, including increased happiness, optimism, self-image and resilience; improved physical health; lower stress levels; enhanced attention, memory, and mental acuity; boosts in positivity; and improvements in overall social and psychological functioning. In our view, all of these benefits stem from an increase in receptivity.

When we asked research participants to describe someone lying in Repose, the most common responses were: "open" and "receptive." Repose places the individual in a state of physical receptivity, which leads invariably to mental receptivity. It does not matter what the person thinks about or keeps from thinking. According to the notion of *somatic feedback* first proposed by William James, the body leads and the mind follows. In the words of Harvard psychologist Amy Cuddy, "our bodies change our minds."[215]

Given enough time, someone lying in Repose will experience psychological repose. This comes more easily with practice, and the beneficial effects can be far-reaching. As Thich Nhat Hanh observes, "We will be more successful in all our endeavors if we can let go of our habit of running all the time, and take little pauses to relax and re-center ourselves."[216] Among these endeavors is creativity. In our research, we have seen evidence of incubation effects with Repose, meaning that people are more likely to solve a challenging problem after a few minutes of Repose than after doing a distraction task (e.g. reading something unrelated to the problem) for the same amount of time.[217]

More significantly, though, I have found that my own creativity has just exploded since I began taking time out for Repose every day. I can feel insights come to me effortlessly while I lie in Repose, and I seem to have more clarity afterwards. Many of the ideas you have encountered throughout this book have come to me in Repose.

I have noticed other indicators of enhanced receptivity, as well. For instance, I seem to be a better listener than I used to be because I allow myself to attend to the other person and to take in what they are saying. And I can relax much more easily in situations that I would have found extremely challenging in the past, such as a trip to the dentist or having blood drawn. Regardless of the situation, I find that now I take more time to assess it before reacting to it.

As with anything else in Deep Creativity, all I can report is my own personal experience. It is up to you to find out for yourself if a technique like Repose can enhance your receptivity and thereby your creativity.

## Self-Transcendence

We already know that self-transcendence is a key element of Deep Creativity. The capacity to move beyond the limits of our minds, egos, and selves makes it possible to connect fully with pure consciousness, the universal mind, and the powerful energies of love and joy. Through self-transcendence, we propel ourselves into the creation cycle. Even if we our only able to transcend ourselves for the briefest of moments, that might be all we need in order to have the kinds of profound insights and realizations that lie at the core of Deep Creativity.

If I had to find one capacity to develop that would enhance not only my creativity but also my overall sense of fulfillment, it would be self-transcendence. That being said, an important question comes to mind: *How do I do that?* The idea that we can train ourselves to be self-transcendent is revolutionary in one sense, and relatively familiar in another. The wisdom of mystics throughout history has focused on this exact task. Mystical teachings all have a slightly different perspective on the challenge of self-transcendence, and yet their messages seem to converge to an extraordinary degree.

Even though I did not grow up Christian, I am intensely attracted to the teachings of Jesus. His message of unconditional love resonates for me. When we love, we transcend ourselves. Virtually all of us have experienced the transcendent nature of love at some point in our lives. Whether it is our love for a friend, pet, spouse, family member, place, or activity, this love is a declaration of sorts. Through our love, we say to the Beloved: *You and I are one. We are not separate. I carry a part of you inside of me.* Now, what can be more self-transcendent than that?

Jesus recognized the power of love, but he also understood that the vast majority of us have hardly begun to tap into that power. It is not enough, he said, to love only a select few. For love to work its transcendent magic on us, we must extend our love to an ever widening circle. In its ultimate form, love can and must encompass everyone and everything.

At this point, let us revisit **Tenet #3: Consciousness is the ultimate source of all creation, including human creativity**. If you accept this tenet, then you realize that there is only one consciousness from which all creativity arises. This consciousness simply adopts myriad perspectives, embodying each of us, looking through our eyes, acting through our bodies, and making sense of the world through our minds. The same Creator abides in you and me. My ability to recognize the Creator in both of us gives rise to a deep sense of connectedness and an inescapable awareness that whatever I am at my core happens to coincide perfectly with what you are at yours.

You and I are one. This is not because we are exactly the same. Each of us has our unique perspectives shaped by our biology, life experience, and distinct selves. But when we learn to look beyond the self—to delve more deeply into the underlying reality—we begin to see the same Creator in all things. Deep Creativity merges into mysticism the moment we begin to experience the Creator within ourselves. When that happens, we embark on a creative and mystical adventure that allows us to see the Creator in others.

This insight leads inevitably and undeniably to unconditional love. What is love, after all, but a deeply-felt sense of communion? When I say, "I love you," I am acknowledging the essential link that exists between us. The Creator in me recognizes the Creator in you. Consciousness is connecting with itself, breaking through the quirky illusion of separateness. The recognition of the Creator in everything around us is a homecoming of sorts. We return to the essence of who we are, which happens to be the essence of all creation. It makes no difference what you say, think, or do. When I direct my attention your way with the understanding that comes from Deep Creativity, I encounter nothing but the Creator. My feelings of love for you are a given and have nothing to do with the superficial circumstances of your life. The Creator has shattered into a billion pieces in large part to experience the pure delight that arises from the act of coming back together again.

Most of us are unfamiliar with unconditional love. We could go our entire lives without encountering it in either ourselves or others. Unconditional love has to be discovered, nurtured and cultivated. Once we have faced and mastered this challenge, limitless avenues of creativity open to us. Why is that? The answer, of course, is that unconditional love is our direct link to the Creator. The whole point of Deep Creativity is to come into the most direct and intimate contact possible with the source of all creation—the pure indivisible consciousness that abides in us and that yields every imaginable breakthrough and revelation. The simplest way to achieve this is by loving everything unconditionally.

So, here is my challenge to you. Make this your mantra: "I LOVE YOU!" Just devote a day, or some large part of it, to moving through the world with these words in mind. Direct them to everyone and everything that enters your field of awareness. You do not need to say the phrase out loud, but you do need to *say it as if you mean it*. At first, you may feel this to be mere pretense. In your heart of hearts, you may know that you do not really feel love for this crack in the sidewalk or that driver who cut you off in traffic. On the other hand, there is something to be said for the philosophy of "fake it 'til you make it." Just telling yourself that you feel love for another increases your chances of actually experiencing it. You are training yourself to see the world through the eyes of the Creator.

Assuming the perspective of the Creator is far from easy, but it is the central task of Deep Creativity. And I would argue that it is also the primary source of fulfillment in our lives. All of the great moments we have ever known—including our most profound experiences of love and joy—have come when we have surrendered our separateness, given in to something far greater than ourselves, and immersed ourselves so thoroughly in this deeper reality that we have disappeared entirely. All that remains at such moments is the pure experience of life and the pure consciousness which is the domain of the Creator. There is only one consciousness that has ever existed or that ever will exist. It is eternal and infinite. The Creator is always there, waiting for us to merge into it. When that happens, we transcend our own mortality and impermanence by arriving at the wellspring of creation, the source and essence of all there is. And this entire transformative process begins with three little words: "I LOVE YOU!"

## Unconventionality

How much of what we think and perceive is determined by our society? This is a pertinent question because the answer can determine our openness to the creative experience. At some point, creativity requires a departure from conventional ways of thinking. Artists have always recognized the importance of their own unconventionality:

> I don't really want to become normal, average, standard. I want merely to gain in strength, in the courage to live out my life more fully, enjoy more, experience more. I want to develop even more original and more unconventional traits.
> —Anaïs Nin[218]

> Human progress has always been driven by a sense of adventure and unconventional thinking.
> —Andre Geim[219]

I've never liked categories. I've never liked boxes. I've always
tried to be unconventional as much as I possibly could.
—Gary Dourdan[220]

The term, *convention*, refers to our customary ways of understanding and interacting with the world. It comes from the Latin "to come together." Members of any society show a great deal of consistency in the ways they make sense of the world around them. This agreement happens through socialization. Certain customs and assumptions are passed down from one generation to the next. As children, we learn to look at people, animals, plants, objects, and events in certain ways. The adults in our lives show us which kinds of behavior are considered proper and improper. They may even set parameters for the range of emotion that we are entitled to experience and display. We discover very early on that there is, in the words of Lyle Lovett, "an acceptable level of ecstasy."[221]

Every waking moment and even in our dreams, our experience of the world is determined to a large extent by convention. The edges we perceive, the distinctions we make, the stories we tell, and the thoughts that preoccupy our minds have been shaped by family, community, and culture. We learn to organize everything into clear categories that allow us to distinguish between human and non-human, male and female, good and evil, animate and inanimate. We categorize people in terms of age, gender, race, religion, ethnicity, sexual preference, political party, and occupation. The use of these categories is useful and practical in many ways, but it comes at a cost, narrowing our awareness and experience of reality.

Convention is a way of *reifying* a thought. The more people agree about a way of thinking or a system of classification, the more concrete and "real" it becomes in their minds. Then, it gets increasingly difficult for any member of their group to depart from the accepted norm. Such a departure represents a challenge to the group's reality, and therefore their identity. As Bertrand Russell observed, "Conventional people are roused to fury by departures from convention, largely because they regard such departures as a criticism of themselves."[222]

But breaking free of convention is a critical task for the artist. In his classic novel, *Madame Bovary*, Gustave Flaubert wrote, "One's duty is to feel what is great, cherish the beautiful, and not accept all the conventions of society."[223] The boundaries imposed by convention are prohibitive; they restrict us to the narrow confines of our own very limited minds. For those of us who seek the expansiveness of the universal mind and the vast range of possibilities it encompasses, there is no choice but to escape the shackles of convention.

In Chapter 1, we identified freshness as one of the two defining qualities of the creative experience. Henri Matisse, one of the pioneers of modern art, considered freshness to be one of the great challenges an artist faces. "The effort to see things without distortion takes something like courage," he wrote, "and this courage is essential to the artist, who has to look at everything as though he saw it for the first time."[224] To experience freshness requires unconventionality. Freshness can only occur when we are not bound by the ways that others have come to view and interpret the world around us. Any conception of the world is going to be too narrow because it draws arbitrary lines around everything. This is done partly to make sense of things, assigning them labels so that we can grasp them and also communicate about them to others. In our pursuit of Deep Creativity, however, we need to be able to look beyond those lines. This is the only way we can get to the underlying essence.

Given that creativity is grounded in unconventionality, is there anything we can do to make ourselves more unconventional? Like every other element of Deep Creativity, the capacity to live outside the accepted social conventions is a matter of choice. First, we recognize the ways that these conventions limit our perspective, and then we make the decision to move past them in the ways we think, act, and experience life. "If you ask me what I came to do in this world," proclaimed Emile Zola, "I, an artist will answer you: I am here to live out loud."[225] To live out loud means to feel things fully, making sure to savor it all—every taste and smell, every moment of beauty, every emotion.

When I moved away from home for the first time at age 18, I decided that I wanted to live the life that was meant for me. I challenged myself not to make assumptions, not to accept the norms, not to do anything simply because that was the way I had always done them. I knew that my decisions up to that point had been made for me largely by others: my parents, friends, grandparents, and teachers. As much as I loved them all, I knew that it was not their place to decide what is best for me. That prerogative belongs only to one person. Only you know what is right for you. As Dr. Seuss may or may not have said, "Be who you are and say what you feel because those who mind don't matter, and those who matter don't mind."[226]

In being true to this challenge, I decided to question everything in my life: what I ate, how I dressed, why I made certain choices, how I spent my time and money, and even whom I considered to be my true friends. Although it was an enormous undertaking, this decision to do what is right for me, regardless of convention, propelled me in the direction that was meant for me—that brings me in alignment with the source of my greatest fulfillment and creative expression.

Disregarding convention does not mean acting in ways that are unethical. I spent much of my youth thinking about ethics. There is a fundamental drive in me, as in you, to do what is right. But what makes a behavior right or wrong? It has never worked for me to behave in certain ways simply because some authority—a higher power, the government, my peers, or Madison Avenue—has dictated it. Instead, I gravitated to the moral philosophy of Immanuel Kant, who offered this categorical imperative: *Act only according to that maxim whereby you can, at the same time, will that it should become a universal law.*[227] I interpreted this to mean that the moral quality of my own behavior could be determined by the answer to one simple question: *What would happen if everyone behaved like this?* If I am acting in ways that I would not want others to emulate, then such action is unethical.

Like everything else in my life, my ethics have evolved. Nowadays, I challenge myself in every interaction to be mindful of one of the central ideas of Deep Creativity: There is only one consciousness, one essence, one Creator. The same consciousness abides in each of us. When I look into your eyes, I try to see the pure consciousness that you and I share. If I fail to see it in you, the onus is entirely on me. Your behavior and intentions should have no impact on me. I make every effort to see the underlying essence in you, as in all beings and all things.

When we aspire to experience life genuinely, we stop taking things for granted. No assumption goes unquestioned. We begin to ask ourselves: Why make this assumption? Is there a more effective approach? What other perspective might shed more light on the situation? How can I enhance my understanding? Why not adopt a different way of thinking or acting? What is keeping me from trying something new here? Is there any reason to think that another approach will not work? And what happens if I do try something different?

Psychologist Erich Fromm observed that "creativity requires the courage to let go of certainties."[228] Our conventions make things seem certain when they are far from it. The certainties of today often turn into the antiquated notions of yesteryear, all because someone had the bold idea to challenge them. At this point, the future of human civilization demands that we question and reinvent virtually everything: our major institutions, spiritual affiliation, economic policies, use of natural resources, moral vision, modes of transportation, population distribution, and relationship to the environment. We can view the interesting times in which we live as either a blessing or a curse. The blessing comes from the opportunity and need for innovation in relation to every aspect of our lives; the curse comes from the consequence of inaction and of holding onto conventions that are destructive rather than productive, limiting rather than uplifting, unjust rather than equitable, and short-sighted rather than visionary.

Beyond the conventional world lies a very different realm—wild, free, and open. Here, we find that anything is possible as long as we can envision it. Jesus said, "Truly I tell you, unless you change and become like little children, you will never enter the kingdom of heaven."[229] The unconventional realm requires a beginner's mind, a cultivated innocence that comes from the realization that we do not know anything about anything—at least not with any kind of certainty. This perspective on the world around us is perfectly captured by Clarissa Pinkola Estés in the following passage:

> Be wild; that is how to clear the river. The river does not
> flow in polluted, we manage that. The river does not dry up, we
> block it. If we want to allow it its freedom, we have to allow our
> ideational lives to be let loose, to stream, letting anything come,

initially censoring nothing. That is creative life. It is made up of divine paradox. To create, one must be willing to be stone stupid, to sit upon a throne on top of a jackass and spill rubies from one's mouth. Then the river will flow. Then we can stand in the stream of it raining down.[230]

# Vision

All creating is becoming. That is one of the bold tenets of Deep Creativity. Before we can become anything, though, we have to envision it. The power of vision is not simply about the use of visual mental imagery. It has everything to do with the ability to conceive of new possibilities. "All the works of man have their origin in creative fantasy," wrote Carl Jung.[231] The evolution of an idea from fantasy to reality is the essence of creative genius.

In the artist's mind, the distinction between fantasy and reality can seem arbitrary. "I'm half living my life between reality and fantasy at all times," noted Lady Gaga, the popular singer, songwriter and actress.[232] Once we envision something, it possesses an element of reality. We say that we *realize* thoughts, words, images, and ideas. What does that mean? By gaining awareness and understanding, we bring these possibilities into existence. To a large degree, we *make* them real. At the very least, they become real for us, whether or not others share in our reality.

When someone else adopts our vision, the reality becomes more tangible. "A dream you dream alone is only a dream," said John Lennon. "A dream you dream together is reality."[233] Everything we interpret as real begins as a vision, a dream, or a fantasy. Even the most basic conception of the world around us—"this is a tree" or "that is the sky"—had to be created by someone at some point in human history. Then it had to be taught and passed down from one generation to the next. Our concepts of *tree* and *sky* are human constructs. You might tell yourself: *But these are tangible realities!* In doing so, you are making the assumption that others are experiencing a tree or the sky in the same way you are. Thankfully, this assumption is not true. The visionary artist or mystic may know them in ways that you cannot even begin to imagine—at least not yet.

William Blake had the remarkable power to look through the surface of things in order to see their true essence. He wrote:

> "What!" it will be questioned, "When the sun rises, do you not see a round disc of fire somewhat like a guinea?" Oh! no, no! I see an innumerable company of the heavenly host crying "Holy, holy, holy is the Lord God Almighty!"[234]

Blake was a true visionary. What makes his vision so remarkable is that it seems to occur so rarely in the general population. Does this mean that such ability is only the birthright of a select few? Of course not! As with any other creative ability, vision has to be nurtured. And the process begins with the kind of unconventionality we have been discussing.

The conventions about reality that our society adopts are not necessarily being imposed or enforced by its wisest or most visionary members. From an early age, we are instructed on the acceptable ways to look at a tree. But as Blake pointed out, "A fool sees not the same tree that a wise man sees."[235] To develop vision, we push ourselves to go deeper. According to Blake, this requires looking *through* our physical eyes rather than with them.

Nothing is ever merely as it seems. We know that appearances can be deceiving, and that the core truth can only be revealed to those willing to go beyond the surface. "There is always a bigger truth undiscovered, unsaid, uncharted, until you meet it," wrote Kimon Nicolaides.[236] Our initial impression of any person, situation, problem, or challenge can be like a cartoon version of reality.

In a Harry Chapin song, a world-weary teacher tells her student, "Flowers are red. Green leaves are green. There's no need to see flowers any other way than the way they always have been seen." Yet I challenge you to look more closely at a leaf or a flower. Can you not see its intricate and multifaceted nature, including all the colors contained in it? The child, whose vision has not yet been suppressed, replies joyfully, "There are so many colors in the rainbow, so many colors in the morning sun, so many colors in a flower, and I see every one."[237]

Jonathan Swift once remarked, "Vision is the art of seeing what is invisible to others."[238] Certain levels of reality remain invisible to us only because we do not take the time to observe, to savor, and to open our hearts to the world around us. If there is only one Creator—one pure consciousness shared by all creation—then *the one that is aware, and the one that abides in awareness, are one.* In this regard, there is little difference between the vision of the artist and the mystic. The Tibetan Buddhist master, Kalu Rinpoche, considered the artist's vision to be an enlightened one, describing it as "a spontaneous expression, just as light radiates spontaneously from the sun without the sun issuing directives or giving any conscious thought to the matter. The sun is, and it radiates."[239]

This vision is inherently about love. To create is to love. Artists immerse themselves in an experience of non-duality, where there is no separation between subject and object, lover and beloved, Creator and creation. We are all capable of such experience, and many of us are already familiar with the non-dual realm. But to move fluidly, consistently, and intentionally into this realm takes an element of vision. If we can envision it, we can experience it

At this point in your life, you may not yet possess such vision. What then? The answer is always the same: *Fake it 'til you make it.* Act as if you are able to see the underlying essence of things, and before you know it, you will be living in that reality. An important part of vision is the capacity for *make-believe*, which is not the same as pretending. When you pretend, you act as if something is true even though you know that it is not. But when you make-believe, first you believe that something is true—or at least possible—and then you make it so. That is the ultimate creative power: You create by becoming, you become by envisioning, and you envision by believing.

If belief and vision are enough to make something real, then why are we not living in a world at peace? We have all seen the bumper stickers urging us to "visualize world peace." Many of us have taken that request to heart. Yet, our world seems far from peaceful. Currently, armed conflicts are taking place in over 50 countries. Millions of pacifists all over the world are envisioning peace, and yet their efforts appear to be ineffective.

Of course, there is no way of knowing how effective these efforts really are. Our world will not become peaceful overnight. But research on mental imagery has shown that it works better to envision a process rather than a result. In other words, instead of trying to visualize a world at peace, we would be better off envisioning the transformative process by which the world becomes more peaceful. What would that process look like? How would it unfold? What resources are needed to make it happen? And what specifically can we do, individually and in concert, to serve as change agents?

Once we have an effective vision in place, then it becomes a numbers game. A new vision of our world moving towards peace must displace the predominant worldview, which accepts intolerance, power struggles, greed, injustice, and antagonism as the norm. An increasing number of us will need to hold this peaceful vision in our hearts and minds in order to make it a reality. As we have already said, reality is nothing more than a common vision. But if we have conflicting visions in the world, the one held by the majority will take precedence. When the lion's share of the global population maintains a vision of peace, the process of realizing that vision will begin to unfold with astonishing rapidity. If you think back to the civil rights movement in the U.S., the end of apartheid in South Africa, the legalization of gay marriage, or the collapse of the Soviet Union, you will see examples of revolutionary changes that gained so much momentum in such a short time that they made a sudden and dramatic leap from impossibility to inevitability.

The final ingredient in the process of realizing a new vision is action. Futurist Joel Barker has said, "Vision without action is merely a dream. Action without vision just passes the time. Vision with action can change the world."[240] We know great artists only through their works. They did not merely envision something; they made it happen. I may think of myself as a would-be inventor because I have conceived of all kinds of new technologies in my head. But until one of those devices actually gets built, tested, and utilized, I will never be a true inventor. When we have a shared vision in place for the pacification of our world, we can begin to act upon that vision, doing whatever is needed to make it happen. Then and only then will this peaceful revolution become our destiny.

That is why Deep Creativity is such a strong passion for me. I know the creative power each of us has at our disposal. We think of individuals like Mahatma Gandhi, Martin Luther King, and Mother Teresa as remarkable, and they most certainly are. What makes them remarkable is their deeply-held vision—not to mention their total devotion to that vision. Each of them shared their vision with such passion and conviction that it eventually became a common reality. The lives of these visionaries exemplify the creative principles we have been discussing here. For each of them, temperament and circumstance came together perfectly, propelling them to action. But without a clear and powerful vision, their impact on the world would never have been felt.

It is hard to look at such individuals and not see pure consciousness, the potent force of love and joy, the heroic journey that is the creative process, and all the elements of the creation cycle coming together to manifest new realities. Now, we redirect our gaze inward, only to find these same elements within ourselves. The same consciousness, energy, and potential that have given rise to the most profound breakthroughs in human history exist within each of us. Martha Graham, the brilliant dancer and choreographer, said it best: "There is a vitality, a life force, an energy, a quickening that is translated through you into action, and because there is only one of you in all time, this expression is unique. And if you block it, it will never exist through any other medium and will be lost."[241]

Your unique vision matters. In fact, it is needed and welcomed. That is why you are here. Inside of you resides a creative force so powerful that it can illuminate the whole world. Yours might very well be the vision that gives rise to a new era of peace, sustainability and balance on our planet. Or it might lead to your own spiritual awakening, which is more than enough. If even one of us "gets the memo," discovering who and what we are at our very core, that can set off a chain reaction far more intense and far-reaching than anything contained in a nuclear reactor. Each of us can be the artist—and our lives the canvas. That canvas is so expansive that it would be a shame to merely confine ourselves to one tiny corner of it. Let us dream big, allowing our creative vision to unfold like a sail in a summer breeze. There need not be any limits to what we can envision or create. "You see things and say, 'Why?'" wrote George Bernard Shaw. "But I dream things that never were, and I say, 'Why not?'"[242]

CHAPTER 13

# Enter the Cycle

*"You can never invite the wind, but you must leave the window open."*
—Bruce Lee

Everyone knows what it feels like to be creative. At some point in our lives, each of us has been drawn to a creative activity. As far back as childhood, we have felt compelled, under the right conditions, to draw, sing, invent, dance, or tell stories. Many of us continue engaging in creative pursuits of some kind throughout our lives. So, you probably have a certain amount of expertise on the topic.

Yet, some of the basic tenets of Deep Creativity may seem foreign to you. Perhaps you have never experienced the pure consciousness of the Creator or the expansiveness of the universal mind. You may have a hard time imagining how such power could even exist within ordinary people, given all of our limitations and frailties. And the very notion of a creation cycle may seem esoteric. How does it pertain to the activities of everyday life?

As surprising as this may sound, the creation cycle has *everything* to do with everyday life. It is relevant not just to your creativity but also to your capacity to learn and to fulfill your potential as a human being. But you cannot just stand on the outside looking in. The creation cycle requires full participation. We have already seen that hero myths offer specific guidance for those seeking to enter into the creation cycle. We also know about the Deep Six, a set of qualities that can open doors into our creative adventure if we choose to nurture and develop them.

The creation cycle resembles a carousel. Once the carousel is in motion, you have to gain momentum to hop on the ride. And this carousel is always in motion! To get on board, you simply need to put yourself in the right position and pick up enough speed. Here, I am going to show you how to do just that, with the help of one of the great visionaries of the Twentieth Century: Bruce Lee.

## The Deep Creativity of Bruce Lee

Yes, this is the same Bruce Lee who starred in a series of actions movies in the early 1970s. Prior to his film career, Lee founded an unorthodox system of martial arts called *Jeet Kune Do* (The Way of the Intercepting Fist). Having trained extensively in various forms of martial arts, he decided these forms were too limiting, and instead developed an approach that was relatively formless and free-flowing. Lee was seeking to break through the rigidity of conventional martial arts in order to allow room for spontaneity and adaptability.

Jeet Kune Do and the philosophy behind it embody many of the principles of Deep Creativity. In his writings, Lee acknowledges the Creator in himself and others. "If there is a God, he is within," he writes. "I feel I have a great creative and spiritual force within me that is greater than faith, greater than ambition, greater than confidence, greater than determination, greater than vision. It is all these combined."[243]

Lee also demonstrates a deep understanding of the relationship between art and mysticism, observing, "Art is the way to the absolute and to the essence of human life."[244] He recognizes the importance of freshness and transcendence, the two defining qualities of Deep Creativity. Much of his focus is on the challenge of cultivating freshness at all times. "Flow in the living moment," he instructs.

"We are always in a process of becoming, and nothing is fixed."[245] Regarding transcendence, Lee focuses on breaking through limitations of every kind: "All fixed set patterns are incapable of adaptability and pliability. The truth is outside of these patterns."[246]

## Emptying and Filling

Seeking to penetrate the creation cycle and the infinite possibilities it holds in store, each of us must begin our journey from within the narrow confines of our individual mind, which Bruce Lee likens to "a finger pointing away to the moon." He warns us not to take this starting point too seriously: "Don't concentrate on the finger or you will miss all that heavenly glory."[247]

We can enter the creation cycle in one of two ways: by *filling* or *emptying*. Filling means taking in the entirety of the universal mind, including all thoughts and all things, whereas emptying goes in the opposite direction, voiding our minds of thought until all that remains is pure consciousness. In one case, we expand our attention to encompass everything; in the other, we narrow our focus until nothing is left.

Lee often uses the metaphor of a cup to describe the individual mind. "Empty your cup so that it can be filled," he claims. "Become devoid to gain totality."[248] But the converse is also true: Fill your cup so that it can be emptied. Consciousness and universal mind are two ends of the same spectrum, and the creation cycle swings—steadily and perpetually—from one end to the other. We can enter the cycle on either end, but if we limit ourselves to what we already know and believe about ourselves and our world, we remain stuck in the middle, much like a pendulum that is waiting to be set in motion.

According to Lee, there is an important distinction to be made between stillness and stagnation. "Only when there is stillness in movement," he notes, "does the universal rhythm manifest."[249] Within the creation cycle, we bear witness to the powerful forces of creation and destruction, as world within world emerges from consciousness and then merges back into it. More than mere witnesses, we become active participants in this eternal dance.

At the core of the creation cycle is the transcendent purity of the Creator-creating-creation. Here is where we want to live, fully connected with the source and essence of our creative power. "Man, the living creature, the creating individual, is always more important than any established style or system."[250] Within this concise statement, Bruce Lee is offering a substantial clue about the nature of our creative power. The source of that power is the Creator-creating-creation, and its essence is our capacity to align completely with the Creator-creating-creation. To come into our creative power as fully as possible, we must avoid getting trapped in "any established style or system." Only by liberating ourselves from the constraints imposed by limited thought processes do we become limitless. And there are two equally effective ways to do this: emptying and filling.

## Emptying

As we discussed in the last chapter, each of us has the capacity for quiescence. By silencing all thoughts, we arrive at pure consciousness. This capacity lies at the core of Lee's teachings. "Empty your mind, be formless," he urges." The knowledge and skills you have achieved are meant to be forgotten so you can float comfortably in emptiness, without obstruction."[251]

This emptying process, as we have seen, depends on absorption: the ability to focus on one thought to the exclusion of all others. Yet, it would seem that total attention to even one thought is a far cry from true emptiness, which is the absence of all thought. How do we go from one thought to none?

An important clue lies in the work of neuropsychologist Roy Pritchard, who developed a type of contact lens that could stabilize an image on a person's retina. In normal vision, the eye is constantly moving. Even when someone tries to fixate on a single visual image, there are small, involuntary eye movements that prevent this from happening. Pritchard's device was like a mini projector that could project an image onto the retina in the exact same location, regardless of how the eye moved. Participants in his studies who were fitted with these contact lenses reported that the image would disappear from view after a few seconds.[252]

Pritchard and his colleagues theorized that sensory receptors in the eye are adapted to detect movement. When an image is held perfectly still, these receptors can no longer detect it. The same appears to be true for the mechanism of attention, which is constantly moving from one thought to the next. If you can hold your attention perfectly still on a single thought for enough time, eventually that thought disappears from awareness. All that remains is pure consciousness, devoid of all thought.

Emptying the mind requires that attention be narrowed more and more until there is only formlessness—the sensation of what Lee calls "the living moment." In this moment, he explains, "life is wide, limitless; there is no border, no frontier."[253] By entering the creation cycle in this way, through the doorway of pure consciousness, you are led invariably to the universal mind. "When one has no form, one can be all forms," notes Lee.[254] Emptying your mind in this way, you join the eternal dance of creation, gaining access to an entire universe of possibility.

## Filling

Now, imagine what would happen if you expanded your attention instead of narrowing it. Here, I will draw a visual analogy. When you look at something—say, a tree in the distance or a cell phone screen a few inches away—you are taking in only a small portion of your entire visual field. If you have a relatively normal visual field, your peripheral vision extends horizontally about 200 degrees and vertically about 150 degrees. That is quite a bit of information that your visual system is able to detect. Yet, at any given moment, you may only be aware of a tiny subset of that field.

Many meditation traditions, including martial arts such as Aikido and Tai Chi, make a distinction between hard and soft gazes. In a hard gaze, the eyes fixate on a specific object or area within the visual field, whereas in a soft gaze, the eyes take in as much of the visual field as possible without focusing exclusively on any one thing. When practicing the soft gaze, you are expanding rather than narrowing your visual attention.

The act of filling is not exclusive to vision. Ask yourself: What would happen if I allowed my attention to stretch as far as it can go, taking in the broadest possible range of thoughts and perceptions? How far could it reach? This is an intriguing thought experiment with major implications. At any given moment, it might be possible for your attention to encompass everything you have ever known—the entire contents of your mind, including all of your memories. And perhaps it could extend even beyond that.

Attention has been likened to a filter or a spotlight, but it is actually more of a gatekeeper. In order to select what gets through to our awareness, it has to judge and evaluate, pick and choose, doubt and reject. There is nothing simple or trivial about the mechanism of selective attention; it has to identify and evaluate all incoming information, at least to a certain degree, before making a decision regarding the salience of that information. The active mode of consciousness, which is the modality in which we spend the vast majority of our time, is dominated by selective attention, which is relentless in choosing what information makes it into our awareness and what gets ignored.

When we shift into the receptive mode, attention takes on a different role. Instead of sorting and selecting, it expands to accommodate more. This can only happen when judgment and evaluation cease. Lee admits, "I am learning to understand rather than immediately judge."[255] In doing so, he is recognizing that judgment restricts what we are capable of knowing. "Reality is apparent when we cease to compare," he claims.[256] Removing the bottleneck imposed by assessment of any kind allows more thoughts to stream into our awareness. In fact, when we stop judging information altogether, the floodgates of attention open wide.

The entire universal mind has always been at our disposal. Through the mechanism of selective attention, we have been letting in a trickle of thought while keeping out an entire ocean. It could be that this mechanism is, to a certain degree, self-protective. Without it, we might experience reality as "one great blooming, buzzing confusion," in the words of William James.[257] Such confusion would surely be inevitable if we tried to make sense of all the information coming at us. But that is not what happens in the receptive mode.

Again, we turn to the distinction between a hard gaze and a soft gaze. Filling means taking in all thought at once just as a soft gaze takes in the entire visual field. The moment we fixate on a single object within our visual field, we are no longer using a soft gaze. And as soon as our attention focuses on a single thought, we shift out of the receptive mode because our attention gets engaged in selection rather than filling. The act of filling is as delicate as dragonfly wings. It requires us to maintain an attitude of total mental receptivity, remaining so perfectly open that we are able to expand our awareness to encompass the entire universe, including all thoughts and all things.

This claim is undoubtedly bold, and it will surely be met with some skepticism. My answer to those who doubt has always been: Try it for yourself! That is why Jhan Kold and I developed Repose. We wanted to offer a simple technique for those who seek to enter the creation cycle through the process of filling. By simply lying in Repose for seven minutes three times a day, virtually anyone can attain the kind of total mental receptivity by which awareness can be expanded.

In one of his poems, Lee writes:

> The doubters said, "Man cannot fly,"
> The doers said, "Maybe but we'll try,"
> And finally soared in the morning glow,
> While the non-believers watched from below.[258]

Filling yourself with the universal mind is very much like flying. You can either stand on the ground wondering if such things are possible, or you can begin to make initial attempts to take off on your own. This does not mean jumping off a cliff without any preparation. We know that Repose and other mindfulness techniques work, and that the condition of total receptivity is not only possible but attainable. Yet, it also takes patience and practice. Just as you might not take off the first time you try flying, it may take several sessions of Repose before you become fully receptive. That is why we suggest giving it at least a month.

To enter the creation cycle in this way is absolutely thrilling. You experience the sensation of taking in an entire universe of possibilities. When this happens, you become formless. In the creation cycle, universal mind leads invariably to pure consciousness, just as consciousness leads invariably to universal mind. As with the act of emptying, all that remains when we fill ourselves completely is the Creator-creating-creation.

## Creativity and Discovery Learning

"Knowing is not enough," Lee maintains. "We must apply."[259] In accordance with this teaching, we will explore an important application of these ideas. We have looked at two ways to enter the creation cycle: emptying and filling. Both of them can be applied to education, for reasons that you are about to discover.

Think about your own learning process. When you are learning something new by discovering it for yourself—a process called *discovery learning*, aptly enough—you can go from ignorance to understanding in a single moment. Suddenly, you gain awareness of new ideas, images, and insights. This expansion of awareness bears a striking resemblance to what takes place during the creative process. There is an important reason for that:

*Tenet #9: Discovery learning and creating are one and the same.*

Like the creative process, discovery learning is defined by freshness and transcendence. When you learn something for the first time, the experience can feel unique and extraordinary because the discovery you are making is new to you, regardless of what others may know. And that discovery pushes you beyond your existing limitations, expanding your knowledge base and giving you an entirely different way of looking at the world.

In Deep Creativity, it makes no difference if the discoveries you make turn out to be familiar to someone else. We define creativity in terms of the process rather than the product. This process is the same for creating and for discovery learning. Both are cyclical in nature. To learn something new, you often have to unlearn bad habits and let go of false assumptions. The process is one of merging and emerging—a constant interplay of form and formlessness, thought and sensation.

Just look at how sensation gives way to thought in discovery learning, which in turn gives way to sensation. When you are fully engaged in this type of learning, the strong sensation of passion can motivate you to delve more deeply into a specific area of interest, just as it would the artist immersed in the creative process. This exploration leads to different kinds of thought—fresh ideas, images, and insights—which in turn inspire other sensations such as the pure joy of discovery or a genuine love for the subject you are learning.

"Life itself is your teacher, and you are in a state of constant learning," writes Lee.[260] The opportunity to engage in discovery learning presents itself at every moment, and these types of opportunities can draw you into the creation cycle. When you throw yourself into discovery learning the way an artist delves into the creative process, you realize that all of the principles of Deep Creativity apply equally to both. Discovery learning, like creating, is an act of becoming. There is only one ultimate source, which is pure consciousness. Love and joy drive both processes. We can think of each as a creative adventure, and the Deep Six are equally pertinent to both.

Whether you are engaged in discovery learning or creating, you can enter the process in the same way: by emptying or filling. This means narrowing your attention until your mind is free of any thought, or conversely, expanding your attention to encompass all thought. Neither approach may seem particularly orthodox, especially in relation to conventional classroom instruction. Most of us were taught that we had to sit up straight and pay attention while a teacher presented information to us. But now, there is growing evidence that this form of instruction is not particularly effective or inspiring, especially in an age when all of us have vast amounts of information at our fingertips.

The word, *education*, comes from the same Latin root as the less familiar *educe*, which means "to bring out or develop." As countless educational theorists have pointed out, the idea of education is to draw something out of us, not to stuff something into us. Ideally, what gets drawn out is our capacity to explore, discover, express, and transcend. According to Lee, "There are no limits. There are only plateaus, and you must not stay there; you must go beyond them."[261]

We all have the capacity to be lifelong learners and creators. Our formal education, to whatever extent we pursue it, has only one objective: To help us transition from dependence to independence—and eventually interdependence. Through our teachers, we can gain the resourcefulness we need to explore our own areas of interest, make our own discoveries, express our thoughts and sensations effectively, and transcend our own limits. At the same time, we also

learn to share and exchange ideas, images, and insights with each other in ways that can benefit all concerned. "Real living," insists Lee, "is living for others."[262]

## Repose and Play

Towards that end, I see a new vision of education: Rather than being told what they need to know, students at all levels can go out and make their own discoveries, driven by the knowledge that learning is creating. In this discovery-based approach, students learn by doing, trying new things and exploring new ideas. The instructor's role is to guide each student's individual learning with a light touch, pointing out alternative strategies that might open new doors, raise new questions, or point to new possibilities. At the same time, students are encouraged to share their exploration with each other, finding areas of common interest and discovering the synergy that comes from cooperation.

Deep Creativity can serve as a resource for students seeking to expand their understanding of the relationship between creativity and discovery learning, as well as their capacity for each. For those who recognize the power contained within the creation cycle, one of the keys to both creating and discovery learning is to unlock that power. This means delving more deeply into the creation cycle. And it all boils down to two tasks: filling and emptying.

I have spent much of my adult life looking for simple ways to accomplish each of these two tasks. In the technique of Repose, I believe that I have discovered one of the most straightforward and effective ways to maximize receptivity so that the act of filling happens spontaneously. Just by lying in Repose, I can feel myself open to the universal mind and all of its contents. This has been such an effective tool for facilitating my own discovery process that I now dream of seeing it incorporated into schools and classrooms throughout the world.

As for emptying, I have looked at thousands of different methods for absorbing attention and emptying the mind of thought. In my second book, *The Way of Play*, I concluded that nothing is more suited to this task than the simple act of play. Any activity that is done for its own sake with no external goal or reward can be considered play and can be used as a tool for emptying the mind. This type of play, which excludes games, sports, or other forms of competition, can be so compelling that we forget about everything else while engaged in it, including our sense of time and even basic needs such as hunger or thirst. Nothing is more absorbing than play. In *The Way of Play*, I wrote, "Meditators dream of attaining the single-minded focus that young children experience naturally when they play."[263]

Imagine what would happen if Repose and play breaks were incorporated routinely into classrooms? Every hour of learning would include at least a few minutes of each. Teachers would begin the period by giving students a specific discovery-based learning task, which could be carried out either individually or in groups. Students would have the opportunity to integrate Repose and play into their learning in ways that would open up their creativity and help them gain a deeper understanding of the challenge at hand. Rather than trying to work longer or harder on a task in order to meet the learning objective, students would discover that they can be more effective by taking breaks at strategic times to either empty their minds or to fill them. Allowing themselves to enter into the creation cycle in these ways, they would be able to make greater strides in their learning with considerably less effort and greater enjoyment.

Perhaps the most important part of learning is self-knowledge. When you discover the ways you learn most effectively, you can begin to work to your strengths and at the same time learn to overcome your weaknesses. Repose and play breaks may not be effective for everyone, but the opportunity to immerse yourself in the creation cycle is likely to be beneficial for you if you try it with patience and dedication. Learning when and how to do so is part of the discovery process. As with anything, only you know what works most effectively as part of your own learning or creative process. As Lee advises, "Adapt what is useful, reject what is useless, and add what is specifically your own."[264]

## Within the Creation Cycle

At the core of the creation cycle is the experience of the creative trinity: Creator-creating-creation. The consciousness from which all thoughts and all things emanate is here at this very moment, writing these words and also reading them. Yet, we may go our entire lives without ever really knowing that we are the Creator-creating-creation. Why is that?

The reason may simply be that we do not have enough proof. If you or I were the Creator, we would expect to be far more creative than we have been up to now. Our creativity may seem somewhat hit-or-miss. In the word of the old Grateful Dead song, "Sometimes the light's all shinin' on me; other times I can barely see."[265] The Creator may abide in you, but that does not make you the Creator. At the same time, you are the Creator, and you are not. How could that be?

Deep within you, the Creator is locked away in a tiny box, much like the genie in the bottle. The security surrounding this box is tight. If you try to break into it, you will find every imaginable obstacle in your way: moats filled with alligators, fire-breathing dragons, minefields and sentries galore. All of these roadblocks were placed there by—you guessed it—none other than yourself. These are the products of your mind: the expectations, judgments, and beliefs that determine everything you know to be true and that prevent you from knowing more.

To set the Creator free, you have no choice but to undertake the kind of adventure described in the world's great hero myths. These stories are metaphorical; the journey is always inward, and the dragons you encounter are of your own making. When he sat under the Bodhi tree to attain enlightenment, the Buddha was engaged in this very undertaking. The demon, Mara, tried to derail his efforts by sending his daughters to seduce him, and when that failed, throwing lightning bolts and fireballs at him. But what exactly was this demon and why was he trying to distract him? You already know the answer. Mara means "mortal one." This is the part of our own psyche that is small, limited, and afraid; that can become susceptible to greed, hate, and delusion; and that blocks our pursuit of self-transcendence because of what it represents.

To our minds and egos, self-transcendence is nothing less than death. The part of us that is mortal also runs from its own mortality. It seeks to escape the inevitable. Obviously, this struggle is destined to fail. Each of us will die sooner or later. Yet, there is something within us that continues beyond this life. That may seem like a bold claim, especially given that human beings have been debating the existence of an afterlife since the beginning of time. So, how can I be so sure?

The answer is simple: I have experienced that which is infinite and eternal within myself, which I call the Creator-creating-creation. There is one consciousness abiding in all of us that can never die because it has never been born. It cannot be extinguished because it has no beginning or end. The Creator transcends everything that our minds can conceive, including the notions of being and nonbeing. When you search for the source of your own creativity, there is nowhere else to look. All categories of thought must arise, ultimately, from a source that transcends them all, and there is only one such source.

The notion of the Creator is just another notion, but it represents the core truth of Deep Creativity. If you cannot accept that truth, you can still engage in the creative process to a certain degree, but your participation and understanding of what is entailed will only take you so far. This is where the scientific approach to creativity hits a wall, failing to recognize the ultimate source of creativity. The more you acknowledge this source, the more deeply you can dive into the creation cycle, and vice versa.

When you immerse yourself completely in the creation cycle, you will have no doubt that the trinity of the Creator-creating-creation abides in you. The creation cycle demands a radical shift in perspective. You go from being a creator to being the Creator. Once this shift has occurred, you see that the entire universe is emerging from your consciousness, which is the only consciousness that has ever existed, and that everything merges back into consciousness eventually.

Most people can buy into the idea that a part of themselves—including a portion of their thoughts and creative energy—gets embedded in the process and products of their creativity. They would probably have no problem making the following statement: *I am the creator of something, and I am in everything I create.* Deep Creativity leads to an important modification of that statement: *I am the Creator, and I am in everything.*

This awareness is the light that guides our pursuit of Deep Creativity. "Those who are unaware they are walking in darkness will never seek the light," says Bruce Lee.[266] He points out that the source of that light has always been within us, but that its discovery requires an element of self-sacrifice. "Now I see that I will never find the light unless, like the candle, I am my own fuel, consuming myself."[267] To enter into the creation cycle, we either fill ourselves with the entire universal mind, or we empty ourselves so that only pure consciousness remains. Either way, we lose ourselves completely in something greater.

# CHAPTER 14

# Beyond Creativity

*"There is no end. There is no beginning. There is only the passion of life."*
—Federico Fellini

Creativity has always been about transcendence. The artist, like the adventurer or mystic, looks to move beyond the familiar in order to experience something fresh and genuine. In the field of Deep Creativity, we take this transcendent impulse to its extreme. That means going beyond everything we know: our beliefs, assumptions, and even our own self-concept. Every aspect of our lives deserves to be questioned and challenged. When we do that, we end up moving so far beyond the spectrum of everyday experience that we find ourselves in a mystical realm.

Consider the words of Abu Yazid Al-Bistami, a Ninth Century Sufi master:

> Nothing is better for a man than to be without anything, having no asceticism, no theory, no practice. When he is without everything, he is with everything.[268]

Our individual minds are limiting. We know this to be the case when we start to comprehend that our creative capacity begins where the individual mind ends. Immersing ourselves in the creation cycle, we experience the purity of consciousness and the expansiveness of the universal mind. Entire worlds of possibility are available to us at such moments. And when we have had that type of experience, even momentarily, there is no denying the fact that we have been grossly underestimating ourselves the whole time we have resisted going there.

More than 12 centuries ago, Zen master Huang Po offered this reminder of what we are, at our very core:

> Your true nature is not lost in moments of delusion, nor is it gained at the moment of enlightenment. It was never born and can never die. It shines through the whole universe, filling emptiness, one with emptiness. It is without time or space, and has no passions, actions, ignorance, or knowledge. In it there are no things, no people, and no Buddhas; it contains not the smallest hairbreadth of anything that exists objectively; it depends on nothing and is attached to nothing. It is all-pervading, radiant beauty; absolute reality, self-existent and uncreated.[269]

Like the hero's adventure, the creative journey leads invariably to apotheosis—the recognition of our own limitless nature. Because of this, we cannot separate art from mysticism. Both pursuits lead to the exact same destination. Perhaps the only difference is that the mystic is more apt to recognize the pursuit and the destination as one and the same, and less likely to be compelled by the need to create. After all, what artifact can begin to capture the perfection of this moment?

## Beyond Convention

In Chapter 12, we looked at the importance of unconventionality. We know that the creative experience unfolds beyond the limits of convention. But how far afield are we willing to go? Is there any convention we are unwilling to relinquish in the name of creativity? Our "sacred cows"—the realities we hold onto with total conviction—have often been imposed on us through the process of acculturation. When we realize that these assumptions are not set in stone and may actually impede our progress, perhaps we may dare to surrender them. Once we do, new vistas open up to us. Suddenly, we are able to see beyond the most distant horizon.

Just consider some of the conventions we have challenged throughout this book:

1.  *The most effective way to study creativity is through the use of scientific methods.* As we have seen, the scientific study of creativity has fallen short in terms of yielding insights into the nature of the creative process. This is partly due to the tendency of creativity researchers to underestimate the role of forces like emotion and intuition in human creativity, and to overestimate the role of logic and inference. In Deep Creativity, we recognize the importance of first-person approaches to the study of creativity. By rejecting such methods as "unscientific," creativity researchers limit severely their ability to shed light on the phenomena they seek to comprehend.

2.  *The creative process is grounded in thought and reasoning.* We have come to understand that creativity is not what we think, and that, in fact, our thinking can interfere with our creative process rather than enable it. As Huang Po said, "When you prevent the rise of conceptual thinking, you will be free men."[270] And freedom, ultimately, lies at the heart of creativity.

3.  *Our individual minds are the source of our creativity.* Here, Deep Creativity departs dramatically from the mainstream. Instead of seven billion different sources of creativity, we attribute all creativity to a single source: the pure consciousness abiding in all human beings and all things. With this one bold leap, we open up new avenues of exploration that unite art and mysticism. For reasons that we have addressed extensively, this is where the study of creativity belongs. It yields important insights into the nature of creativity that we would never be able to access otherwise.

4. *Creative genius is the birthright of a select few.* A great deal has been written on the topic of eminence, which is the recognized superiority of certain individuals, especially with respect to creativity. Although there is no denying that some people excel more than others in every field, we do not attribute this success to some innate creative ability that is distributed unequally in the population. One of the most important assertions of Deep Creativity is that each of us has equal access to the universal mind, which encompasses all thoughts and all things. Tapping into this limitless reservoir of ideas and possibilities has more to do with passion and determination—qualities that virtually anyone can cultivate—than with innate ability.

5. *Thoughts and things are created differently.* Scientists have treated human creativity as distinct from the creative processes taking place throughout the natural world. In fact, they have overlooked the similarities almost entirely. In Deep Creativity, we take a different approach, treating things "out there" and thoughts "in here" as interrelated. Both exist within the domain of the universal mind, and each undergoes a cyclical process, emerging from consciousness and then merging back into it. The same creation cycle that we observe in nature lies at the heart of human creativity. Attempts to impose linearity on the creative process have failed because they give an incomplete picture of what is taking place.

6. *The most important aspect of human creativity is the final product.* In a results-oriented society, there is a tendency to focus on end results. The private sector in particular is drawn to the topic of creativity because of its potential to boost productivity. But the cyclical nature of the creative process means that there can never be a "final" product. The creation cycle perpetuates itself infinitely. The product of one round of that cycle is also the starting point for the next. In Deep Creativity, we are far more interested in the process than the product, and our ultimate priority is the transformation experienced by anyone who chooses to take part in that process. Those of us who set out on our creative adventure have the opportunity to merge into pure consciousness and to know the perfect joy of creation.

# Beyond Space and Time

At the outset, we defined the creative process in terms of two characteristics: freshness and transcendence. Those two qualities drive us to go ever deeper in our creative pursuits. Like any emerging field of endeavor, Deep Creativity pushes us constantly to challenge existing assumptions. We do this not because we think that newer is necessarily better, but because we know that the experience of freshness and transcendence cannot be contained within any conceptual framework.

Throughout this book, we have broken through some basic conventions, and not just the ones pertaining to creativity. We have proposed a radical view of the universe that includes the following elements: a unitary consciousness embedding itself in all of creation; the access of each individual to a universal mind; the equivalence of thoughts and things; the creative power of love, joy, ecstasy and bliss; and the cyclical nature of the creative process.

Yet, we ask ourselves: Can we go even deeper? Our commitment to the qualities of freshness and transcendence demands that we continue questioning even our most fundamental assumptions about the universe, starting with our understanding of space and time. What happens when we transcend the idea of three-dimensional space? Instead of thinking of each object as occupying its own unique position in space, we can consider the possibility that everything is *coterminous*. Our sense of physical separation may very well be illusory. What if everything in the universe were right here, occupying a place within our perceived reality? If all things are ultimately thoughts, and all thoughts abide within the universal mind, then our ability to access this mind allows our awareness to encompass everything that exists in three-dimensional space. Under the right circumstances, we can expand our minds simultaneously into every corner of the universe.

Then there is the notion of time. When we transcend it, we discover that we are living in perfection. This moment is simply perfect, meaning that it encompasses all points in time. Everything is present in the present. The past is here, imprinting itself on this moment. In fact, the past only exists to the extent that it influences our thoughts, feelings, and behavior right now. Otherwise, how would we know that the events of the past ever took place?

Those who came before, including our loved ones that have died, must be here with us. Even if we are not thinking of them right now, they are shaping our experience. Think of all the ways the person you are right now has been molded by someone important in your life, such as a parent, grandparent, or mentor: by watching their behavior, hearing their words, sharing a living space and possibly genetics with them, observing how they live, emulating them, judging them, loving them, and even hating them. Physical death cannot deny these individuals the capacity to maintain their presence in this moment, through us.

As for the future, you already know what I am going to say: It is nothing but a dream. We bring the future into being by envisioning it—in the present moment. The future resides in the clouds, within our own imagination. When the future does arrive, as we are predicting it will, then it becomes the present. That is the most obvious of assumptions, right? But maybe the future is always here with us, a part of our mental landscape. The dream world of our imagination is very much a part of the perfection of this moment. How could it not be? And most of its contents pertain to this hypothetical thing called *the future*.

If the future exists as part of the perfection of the moment, then the things we are going to create or become are here now. The transformations we expect to undergo must already exist. These changes are unfolding and have unfolded—at least to the extent that we have imagined they will. Nothing can be created that is already present. At the same time, nothing can be destroyed if its presence can still be felt.

To live in perfection means to be aware of the completeness of the moment. We become mindful of the fact that everything we could ever want or need is here. There is nothing else we need to be, do, or have. We feel wholly satisfied with whatever experience there is to be had right now. Why look beyond this moment by either reliving the past or anticipating the future, unless doing so enhances our present? For those of us who enjoy planning, thoughts of the future can enrich our lives. But planning for the future only makes sense for those who are living in the perfection of this moment. After all, if someone does not know what it feels like to experience the fullness of the present moment, then they will probably never know the fullness of future moments, either. That being the case, why plan for something that you will never get to experience, let alone enjoy?

I would go so far as to say that the only point of being alive is to seize the opportunity to live in perfection. To know that this moment is perfect, and to bask in its sweetness, can be considered our greatest success. And to feel that something is lacking can be our greatest failure. We can get caught in the trap of thinking "*if only.*" We may tell ourselves that everything would be perfect *if only* something had happened differently in the past or that everything will be perfect *if only* something could happen differently in the future. In holding out for more, we miss out on the abundance that already exists in the here and now.

Even one moment of living in perfection is enough. Think about it: If everything is contained in this moment, then the experience of it gives us complete knowledge of all that ever was or will be. Being fully present right now, we become infinite and eternal. The entire universe is contained in the space we occupy, and all of posterity in the instant that we come to life, as William Blake stated so eloquently:

> To see a World in a Grain of Sand
> And a Heaven in a Wild Flower
> Hold Infinity in the palm of your hand
> And Eternity in an hour [271]

## Beyond the Creative Trinity

Like any other field of endeavor, Deep Creativity offers a conceptual framework that can help us come to terms with reality. But any such framework can also restrict our range of experience. For anything that we can conceive, there is always something more. To illustrate, I would like you to envision the universe. That seems like a ridiculous task. How can anyone capture the expansiveness of the universe in a single thought or image? No matter how far you stretch your notion of the universe, you know that it cannot extend far enough. The same is true of concepts like infinity, eternity, or perfection.

Now, consider the creative trinity: Creator-creating-creation. Is there any doubt that each of the concepts comprising this trinity alludes to something that transcends mental boundaries? We have described the Creator as pure consciousness embedding itself in all things—at every level of the universe from the infinite to the infinitesimal. The Creator is both immanent and transcendent. This is a paradox too profound to fathom. We have no chance of wrapping our limited minds around it. So, our tendency is not to try. But just because we are unable to grasp the profound nature of the Creator does not mean that we should dismiss it altogether. Rumi likened our mental struggle with this notion to that of an embryo just learning about the vast world outside the womb. Here is the embryo's first reaction: "There is no 'other world.' I only know what I've experienced. You must be hallucinating."[272]

The Creator is too expansive and pervasive to be captured within any conceptual framework. So, how can we be sure that the Creator even exists? It might just be the hallucination of a delusional mind. But I happen to know the existence of the Creator with absolute certainty. Here is how I know: The Creator is reading the words on this page at this very moment! The fact that you can say, "I am," confirms the existence of this pure consciousness abiding in all things. And so, whether you believe me or not, I still have no choice but to bow to you, recognizing something in you that you may not even recognize in yourself—at least not yet.

The second element of the creative trinity is the act of creating. When we transcend the concepts of space and time, we begin to understand that, ultimately, there can be no creative act. The present moment is perfect, complete, and absolute. *Everything that ever was or ever will be is here right now.* That being the case, nothing can be created—or destroyed, for that matter. All we can do is illuminate our own individual minds by shining the beacon of awareness on something that has been there all along, residing in the shadows.

Finally, there is the element of creation. This is the sum total of everything encompassed in the universal mind, including all thoughts and all things. Deep Creativity challenges the conventional distinction between the physical and mental realms. We have seen that thoughts and things are interchangeable in many respects. More importantly, we recognize that we are living in a realm of thought, which means that the reality we perceive is ultimately a mental construct. Only through our thought processes does physical reality exist at all.

When we become aware of something, the pure consciousness abiding in us is simply acknowledging itself in the object of our awareness. The fact that the Creator can be found in everything, including our own minds, leads to this important conclusion: *The one that is aware, and the one that abides in awareness, are one.* Ironically, this identity holds true, whether we are aware of it or not. Each of us determines what we allow into our awareness. In making the determination, we are constantly engaged in a type of creative process. By drawing something into our awareness, we identify with it at a fundamental level. We are creating by becoming. The more explicitly we do this, the more we come into our own, not just as creative entities but as human beings.

Creativity exists only from the human perspective. Human beings alone can bring something into existence by bringing it into awareness. The Creator exists in all things, as it always has. So, how can it create by becoming? What can the Creator become that it has not already been? Yet, by embedding itself within our individual minds, the Creator can direct awareness to only some small part of the universe while disregarding the rest. It can experience the illusion of separateness, of individual identity. Only in human form can the Creator impose limitations and divisions, drawing distinctions between self and other. Ironically, it is this limited nature of our individual minds that allows us to create. We can only have the experience of becoming something that we have not yet been. Our self-imposed limitations give us the capacity to transcend and to create.

## Mindfulness and Disinhibition

You and I can bring any or all of creation into being simply by drawing our attention to it. When something enters into our awareness, it merges into the Creator abiding in us. Once that happens, we have created by becoming. The Creator can only create through us. The experience of creating happens the moment we become aware of something. This experience is not limited to the first time something enters our awareness.

Suppose you are tasting the juicy sweetness of a strawberry as you bite into it. Now, you may have tasted strawberries many times before. Keep in mind that when it comes to the creative experience, novelty does not matter. The two criteria we have identified for creativity at the level of process are freshness and transcendence. If you are aware of the strawberry *as if* for the first time, it makes no difference that you may have already bitten into a dozen other strawberries in the past few minutes alone. The experience of *this* strawberry is the only thing that matters. If your awareness of it feels fresh and transcendent, then you are creating the *strawberry experience* at this very moment.

That is why mystics and artists alike have stressed the value of mindfulness. When we bring something into our awareness fully, we are creating it in a very real sense. It does not matter one bit whether or not that thing has existed before. The past is irrelevant to those of us living in perfection; we realize that it exists only as part of the present moment. Our mindfulness can create anything that can be encompassed in our awareness. This is our most precious gift. We extend our awareness as far as it can reach, and then entire universes come into being.

Mindfulness is not simply a matter of breadth. We do not need to push our awareness out to the far reaches of the cosmos, although that in itself is a wonderful exercise. Just as powerful is the act of focusing attention entirely on the tiniest bit. Remember that the universal mind is a fractal: *The source is entangled in the universe, layer upon embedded layer.* Even the most minute object or entity contains infinite layers, each of which is imbued with the same pure consciousness that illuminates our own minds. When we are mindful of anything at all, the Creator in us reunites with itself in the object of our awareness. Besides giving rise to the experience of creation, these moments should be cause for celebration. We are expanding our awareness beyond the boundaries of our very limited individual minds, and reconnecting with pure consciousness, which is our essential nature.

The opposite of mindfulness is mindlessness. We can move through the course of our day without being fully aware of anything. This is the prerogative of every human being. Each of us has a gift; we can create whatever we want simply by drawing it into our awareness. Or we can choose not to deploy our awareness at all. Amos Tversky, whose research on cognitive bias led to a Nobel Prize in Economics, once told me, "The only thing that matters is what's on your mind—not what's in it."[273] By this, he meant that when it comes to how we respond to the present moment, mindfulness is more important than intelligence or education. Tversky spent his career studying the ways that mindlessness results in poor judgment and decision-making. He realized that we can only go as far as our awareness will take us, here and now. Our knowledge base has no value if we cannot draw upon it when we need it.

This leads to a very simple and useful heuristic: *If you want to be more creative, be more mindful.* Explore the richness that surrounds and fills you. There is no distinction to be made between inner and outer reality—not when it comes to our own creativity. Anything and everything is deserving of our attention. Whatever inspires us is inherently inspiring. It hardly matters if anyone else shares in our inspiration, though the chances are good that something which triggers excitement and passion in us will have a similar effect on someone else.

Many years ago, I made this silent pact with everyone I would ever encounter: *Show me what you love, and I will love it.* If even one person I meet finds inspiration in a particular subject, I must make every effort to discover what it is that makes the subject so inspiring to him or her. My inability to see the inherent beauty of that subject reflects entirely on me. Only my own limitations keep me from appreciating it. "Every failure to cope with a life situation," wrote Joseph Campbell, "must be laid, in the end, to a restriction of consciousness."[274]

All restrictions on our consciousness are self-imposed. We tend to reign in our awareness rather than turn it loose. Some researchers have linked creativity to *cognitive disinhibition*, which is the ability to pay attention to what others ignore. We fear this ability because we know that it can lead to madness. There is no question that disinhibition has a positive association with psychopathology. But the challenge for individuals with mental health issues such as schizophrenia is to try and reign in their attention, which is the opposite end of the spectrum from the majority of us, who tend to keep our attention on a very short leash. If we give the leash a little more slack, we are unlikely to go insane. Instead, we increase our chances of seeing things in entirely new ways, gaining fresh insights and discovering subtleties that we may have missed before.

## Creating the Creator

We can create an entire universe through the power of awareness. Given that all creating is becoming, and that our awareness allows us to become one with the object of our awareness, it follows that when we become aware of something, we are engaged in the act of creation. This is the same power possessed by the Hindu god, Brahma, who brings a world into being simply by opening his eyes.

So, what happens when we direct our awareness to the Creator, either in ourselves or in others? This is a profound question, indeed. Its implications would be that we tiny human being can give rise to something so enormous and far-reaching. But can we really create consciousness itself, which is the source and essence of all things? The Creator may be what logicians call a *first principle*—a fundamental assumption that cannot be derived from anything else. Is the Creator not the starting point for everything we know? If so, how can we possibly create it?

The 13th Century German mystic, Meister Eckhart, offered a perfect answer to these questions:

"The eye through which I see God is the same eye through which God sees me; my eye and God's eye are one eye, one seeing, one knowing, one love."[275]

There is and only ever has been one consciousness, which resides in you as in me as in all things. By embodying you, consciousness can create universe upon universe, all from inside of you. Then, when you become aware of the Creator within you, the Creator *is creating* the Creator within you. So, what does this all mean? Is the Creator within you just a mental construct? Yes and no. When we assign it a label and attempt to write or talk about it, we are undoubtedly working with a mental construct. This is the handle our minds use in order to try and grasp something that is not perfectly graspable.

But is there more to the Creator than the mental construct? The question itself makes me want to burst out laughing. I laugh only with delight—never out of ridicule. There is so much more to the Creator that it staggers the mind to even attempt to comprehend it. All I can say is: "Let go." If you get out of your own way, you will find how much more there is to experience and discover. You and I have the ability to remove ourselves from our own awareness. The person we know ourselves to be simply disappears, going away completely for a period of time. In fact, time itself becomes irrelevant because we can make that disappear, as well. Space, too. We are even able to take the Creator out of the equation. So, what is left?

Again, we turn to Meister Eckhart, who describes this ability as *poverty of spirit* and considers it perhaps our greatest virtue:

Poverty of spirit means that a man is so empty of God and of all his works that if God wants to act in the soul, he himself must be the place where he wants to act—and this he does gladly. For if he finds a man as poor as this, then God alone acts and the man allows God to act in him, and God is his own place of activity, because God is acting in himself. It is here, in this poverty, that a man attains the eternal essence which he once was and which he now is and which he will forever remain.[276]

And so, we arrive at the last and perhaps most important of our Ten Tents:

## Tenet #10: Only the contents of our minds change as the result of the creative process.

Throughout the creative process, this is all that ever changes. Our minds can become infinite, taking in all that is encompassed within the universal mind. Or they can disappear entirely, merging so completely with pure consciousness that nothing else remains. When that happens, all that exists is the eternal dance of essence and non-essence, which can only be known through direct experience. The splendor of this dance cannot be described adequately, even though I can hardly resist attempting to do so. Why do I have problems resisting this urge? Simply because talking, writing, or thinking about it has a way of leading me into the experience.

I am referring to the experience of transcendence, which wipes away every bit of our knowledge, including that of our individual identity. Once this slate is wiped perfectly clean, a void remains to be filled. From the perfect unity of the Creator emerges the multiplicity of the universal mind. The creation cycle is set in motion in perpetuity: death and rebirth, merging and emerging, on and on it goes.

Before Deep Creativity, the focus of those who studied creativity had been on creative products—the ideas and insights that stick to our individual minds as a result of the creative process. These products are intriguing to us, because they have a way of shaping the contents of our minds. When we interact with a great work of art or use a new technology, our lives can be changed irreversibly. In this way, creativity breeds more creativity. The contents of your mind help determine the contents of my mind, which exert an influence on someone else's mind. This can continue ad infinitum.

Yet, there is something far more compelling to be found by focusing on the process itself rather than the products. Through this process, we immerse ourselves in love and joy, ecstasy and bliss. And then we go beyond that. We stretch ourselves until we are infinite and eternal. And then we go beyond *that*. We uncover worlds hidden within worlds. And then we go beyond *that*. We find out what it is like to be the Creator-creating-creation. And then we go beyond *that*. We disappear into the unity of essence and the void of non-essence. And then we go beyond *even that*.

We undertake a creative adventure that never ends, that just keeps going deeper and deeper into the true nature of all that is. This journey extends far beyond our lifespan or the scope of our individual minds. Just when we think that it has reached its peak or culmination, the journey continues to take us to new depths, greater heights, and farther reaches. No matter where it leads us, this beautiful, joyous creative adventure continues to open new vistas for us, pushing us ever onward: Beyond, beyond, always beyond.

# CHAPTER 15

# Greatness

*"The story of the human race is the story of*
*men and women selling themselves short."*
—Abraham Maslow

March 16. 1987. The inspiration for this book came in the form of a powerful inner voice, delivering a message that has had a profound and lasting impact on my life. I was staying on Fitzroy Island, a halfway point between the Australian coast and the Great Barrier Reef. My passion for coral reefs had gotten me this far, but I was about to discover the real reason for my journey. I had to travel halfway across the world to find something that I had been carrying inside of me all along.

While staying in a small youth hostel, I decided to go for a moonlight swim in a protected inlet. As I floated on the gentle ocean waves, looking up at the constellations of the Southern sky, I wondered what I was doing so far from home. At the age of 27, I had left everything behind—my home, friends, family, and career—to go on an adventure through the South Pacific. The Great Barrier

Reef had been my ultimate destination, but I wasn't sure why I had become so obsessed with it. As I reflected on the nature of my journey, a strange sensation came over me. I had a sense of foreshadowing—a vague feeling that something important was about to happen.

After my swim, I went back to my dorm room and tried to sleep. The room felt stuffy and confining, and it seemed like hours before I could get comfortable on the rickety bed. Finally, I managed to fall asleep, only to be awakened a short while later by a powerful male voice.

"You are greater than you ever imagined," it said in the darkness.

I ran over to the wall and turned on the light. At that moment, the largest spider I had ever seen raced across the room, under the door, and out into the hallway. I actually followed it, wondering if somehow this spider was the one who had spoken to me. There was certainly nobody else around. After a few minutes, it crawled into a neighboring room and I had no choice but to abandon my chase.

By the time I got back into bed, I was beginning to wonder if it had just been a dream. The words had been so vivid, though, that they felt real. Unlike any other dream I had ever had, there were no visual images. I lay in bed and just repeated the words to myself. With each repetition, I grew more excited as the significance of the statement began to dawn on me.

*You are greater than you ever imagined.* There was something so beautiful and profound about these words. They let me know that I was connected to something limitless and all-encompassing. As I repeated them to myself, I could sense a door of some kind opening for me. I began to realize how much I had been underestimating myself—and people in general. No matter how high you set the bar, in terms of your expectations of what people are capable of being, doing, thinking or feeling, it seems that someone somewhere is able to exceed it. So, why do we tend to set the bar so low?

At that moment, I knew that a crime had been committed against humanity. The tendency to underestimate our own capabilities is perhaps the greatest conspiracy in human history. Ironically, we are all complicit in it. The conspiracy is self-perpetuated; we learn to limit ourselves at an early age, and then we pass along these self-imposed limitations to the next generation.

I recalled one of my favorite quotes, from physicist David Bohm: "Whatever we know of the world, there is always more."[277] This statement seemed particularly true of the human spirit. In my travels, I had met hundreds of remarkable individuals who had astounded me with their generosity, resourcefulness, talent, selflessness, resilience, and—most of all—creative ability. On an almost daily basis, I crossed paths with inventers and investors, musicians and magicians, healers and dealers, schemers and scammers, all of whom shared their stories of redemption and reinvention. I gravitated to those intrepid souls who were trying to carve out a path where none had existed before. Their lives were their art; starting with an empty canvas, each of them was attempting to create a masterpiece.

My encounters with these individuals had given me a glimpse of the greatness inherent in each one of us. Now, I had a surge of energy go through my body as I was filled with an overwhelming desire to understand this inner greatness. At that moment, I knew my travels were over. It was time to turn back and head home. I had been ready to end my trip for several weeks, and yet something had compelled me to keep going. Here I was, seven thousand miles from home and finally I understood why I had come this far. I had been on a pilgrimage of sorts—a quest for the central vision of my life that would focus my energy and direct my actions. Now I had what I wanted, in the form of a simple seven-word statement: *You are greater than you ever imagined.*

Two years later, I enrolled in a Ph.D. program in psychology at the University of Arizona. I came to the desert with the intention of learning everything I could about greatness. In a very real sense, then, this book has been nearly 30 years in the making. Part of the reason it took so long is that I had to find my way in the dark. Few scholars have explored this notion—at least not in the way I have experienced it. Only since the start of the new millennium has the field of psychology even made it a priority to focus on the positive side of human nature, including the various aspects of well-being.[278] There is very little the field has discovered about the kind of greatness to which I am referring.

## Being and Doing

When I began investigating this question of greatness, I discovered the biases not just of psychologists but of our society in general. We tend to focus on power, achievement, wealth attainment, technological innovation, and excellence in competition. As I have said before, we are undoubtedly living in a results-oriented society. Yet the prevailing understanding of greatness simply did not resonate for me. I knew from the outset that there was something more. I began to gravitate to the work of Abraham Maslow, who was concerned with self-actualization and peak experiences.

We are all familiar with peak experiences because we have had them in the course of our lives. At certain moments, we have felt the exhilaration that comes from being fully alive, completely engaged in the present, totally immersed in whatever we are feeling or doing. Over the years, I have done informal research with the people I meet, asking them to describe their peak experiences to me. Part of the reason I do this is that I am inspired by their inspiration: *Show me what you love, and I will love it.*

But another reason is that the field of psychology has come to an enormous misconception about the nature of peak experiences. In recent years, researchers have confounded peak experiences with *flow*, a particular type of experience in which "a person performing an activity is fully immersed in a feeling of energized focus, full involvement, and enjoyment in the process of the activity."[279] Flow is characterized by the kind of task one is doing, which needs to be challenging, and the degree of perceived skill one needs to have, which must be high. The emphasis here is on *doing* rather than *being*.

This shows the bias of the researchers, who are themselves achievement-oriented. But their bias does not seem to align with reality. Once the people who took part in my study had described a peak experience for me, I asked them the following question:

> Which of the following is a more accurate descriptor of your response to the situation?
> 1. DOING-Fully engaged in an activity
> 2. BEING-Fully receptive to an experience

Over two-thirds of them chose BEING over DOING. They also rated their experience as being relatively low in terms of the level of challenge imposed by the situation and the level of skill required of them. I had a wide range of peak experiences described to me, which included: holding one's newborn baby for the first time; lying in a field watching clouds go by; jumping out of an airplane; adopting a puppy; riding on a rollercoaster; watching a sunrise or sunset; a trip to the ocean; a first kiss; seeing a natural wonder like the Grand Canyon; and reuniting with a loved one after a long absence. This is just a small sampling of the stories I have had the privilege to hear or read. There is so much beauty and power in them that I could easily spend a lifetime just asking people to share these types of experiences with me.

What matters here is that people are moved much more by an experience than an activity. Process matters far more than product. In these stories, there is rarely a goal to be attained or a challenge to overcome. For most of us, greatness does not lie in accomplishment but rather in deeply-felt sensations and emotions. The scientists who study flow claim that situations presenting little or no challenge and requiring little or no skill lead to apathy and boredom. This is so far from my own experience—or most people's, for that matter—that I cannot begin to understand how these researchers have managed to steer so far off-course.

## Experiencing Greatness

I have no intention of telling you what greatness should mean to you. Greatness is whatever you want it to be, and it lies wherever you find it. If something moves you greatly, then you have found greatness. You may discover that you are touched most deeply at some particular level more than any other. This level could be emotional, intellectual, sensual, sexual, spiritual or visceral. However you get there, greatness happens when you feel completely enlivened, as if you have just been born into the world and are experiencing everything for the very first time.

Through this experience, we may discover greatness in three distinct ways:

1. By being aware of it. This involves recognizing and embracing whatever it is that moves us and draws us into the experience in the first place.

2. By creating it. We can capture greatness in our thoughts and actions so that others may share in our experience.

3. By becoming it. Whatever it is that moves us is also something we can embody and manifest.

Given these three paths to greatness, it should come as no surprise that my pursuit of greatness led me to the study of: 1) consciousness; and 2) creativity. Deep Creativity is the intersection of these two topics. But there is a third component, as well. What could it be? It has something to do with our ability not just to experience and create greatness but to actually *become* it.

After spending years chasing down the elusive third element of Deep Creativity, I arrived at an important realization: It is *unconditional love*! We have already addressed the topic of unconditional love, perhaps more than any other creativity book ever written. Researchers are not particularly comfortable with this topic, which is far too intimate and "touchy feely." Perhaps they do not understand its connection to creativity. It took me years to grasp its relevance. But once I did, I realized that no conception of the creative process can be complete without it.

Unconditional love does not come easily. Mostly, we love what is pleasing to us. After all, who loves cockroaches? Charles Manson? Or cancer? To love unconditionally means to recognize the Beloved in someone or something, and then to merge completely with the Beloved: one body, one mind, and one heart. The Beloved can be anything or anyone you want it to be. In unconditional love, you accept the Beloved as yourself, and you do so completely. You know what the Beloved knows. You feel what the Beloved feels. If the Beloved is a person, you accept as your own the thoughts and actions of the Beloved. This is a particularly huge challenge.

Why do friendships and intimate relationships end? Usually, someone says or does something that the other person cannot accept. The two individuals are not of one mind, and so the love they share is not unconditional. This is not a judgment. It is simply the reality that unconditional love challenges our very notion of what it means to love. Is there anything or anyone on this Earth that you love so completely that all separation between yourself and the Beloved ceases to exist? If so, your love is unconditional. But if not, unconditional love may be as elusive for you as it is for the vast majority of us.

## Creativity and Unconditional Love

So, where does unconditional love fit into our discussion? In the last chapter, we reached a startling conclusion:

*Tenet #10: Only the contents of our minds change as the result of the creative process.*

Consciousness, which abides in us as in all things, never changes; it remains pure, formless, and transcendent. The universal mind does not change, either; it encompasses everything that ever was, is, or will be.

Creativity is our unique privilege and birthright. The individual mind is the only entity in the entire universe that creates by becoming. This statement may seem to contradict **Tenet #3: Consciousness is the source of all creation, including human creativity**. But in reality, there is no conflict. Without consciousness, there can be no individual mind. Consciousness is our essence and fundamental nature, inextricably linked to everything we know, think, and feel. How could it not be the source of our creativity?

Yet, pure consciousness does not create anything on its own. Through the creation cycle, the universal mind emerges from consciousness and merges back again. Within this mind is contained all form, a subset of which is accessible to our individual minds. The very quality of our minds that limits us also allows us to create. We determine what it is that enters our awareness, and this determination holds the key to our creativity.

Our minds create by becoming, and they only become by being aware. This statement should not come as any surprise. We know that the creative process is transformative. That was stated in **Tenet #2: All creating is becoming**. Sometimes we become the character we are bringing to life, the brush strokes we are applying to the canvas, or the lines of poetry that come through us. Our creations became a part of us. Every day, I live joyfully with the things I have created, including the music I have composed and the practical ideas I have generated. I do so with complete humility, because I never have a moment of doubt about the ultimate source of it all. The Creator enlivens my awareness and inspires my every thought. Although I play an active role in the creative process, I also know that when it comes to the actual moment of revelation, I am just along for the ride. Consciousness and the universal mind imbue me with ideas and insights that may be new to me, and perhaps even to others, but that have always existed somewhere in the universe.

The second part of the statement—"we become by being aware"—should have a certain degree of familiarity as well, although it is undoubtedly radical in its implications. In the last few chapters, I have introduced you to this profound notion: *The one that is aware, and the one that abides in awareness, are one.* The same consciousness that abides in us also abides in that which occupies our awareness. So, when we turn our awareness to something—anything at all—we are drawing that object of awareness into ourselves, becoming one with it.

You have every right to stop and challenge this assertion. Perhaps you may think: *I am often aware of something in my surroundings without feeling any particular connection to it.* In fact, you may not feel a connection to the vast majority of people and things that penetrate your awareness. I am not asserting that the identification between the subject and object of awareness will always be perceived consciously: only that this identification exists at some level. The only way to know this connection explicitly is through the power of unconditional love.

Now, you can begin to see the relevance of unconditional love to the creative process. The force of unconditional love allows us to expand ourselves in such a way that we merge with another entity. We do not simply bring that entity into our awareness; we incorporate it into ourselves. Unconditional love inspires this simple realization: *The Beloved and I are one.* By merging into the Beloved, we transcend our own separateness and create the Beloved within ourselves. This is an extraordinary power that we all possess, but that most of us will hardly ever use. Unconditional love can set in motion the entire creation cycle.

# The Beloved Creator

The Beloved can be anything or anyone you want it to be. So, imagine that the Beloved is the Creator in its entirety: pure consciousness, the universal mind, and creative energy. What if you could love the Creator so unconditionally that you were to experience total communion? You would recognize the Creator as the Beloved, and you and the Beloved would be one. You would accept as your own everything about the Beloved: consciousness and mind, love and joy, ecstasy and bliss.

The biggest obstacle to this leap would be your own judgment. To love something unconditionally is to accept everything about it. The Creator abides in absolutely everything: the desirable and undesirable alike. When it comes to unconditional love, you cannot pick and choose. When you label something as "evil" or "repugnant," that takes you completely out of the experience.

We often stand in judgment of the Creator, questioning the fairness of it all. There are times when we may wonder why the events in our lives had to play out the way they did, or if it would have been better for things to turn out differently. In the film, *Fearless*, the Catholic mother, Carla, whose son has just died in a plane crash that she survived, tells her fellow survivor, Max, "You know He hurt me. He hurt me forever." Max replies, "People don't so much believe in God as they choose not to believe in nothing. Life and death…they happen for no reason."[280]

We call this a "crisis of faith," but perhaps it is more a *crisis of love*. When we love unconditionally, we accept the Beloved entirely into our hearts. There is no separation. We do not reject or disregard the Beloved when things do not go our way. That type of reaction represents an incomplete or underdeveloped capacity to love.

Unconditional love is hard, without a doubt. To merge completely with the Beloved requires an open-heartedness that few of us have ever allowed ourselves to experience. We must be willing, eager, and even delighted to give ourselves completely to the Beloved, and to receive the Beloved completely. Unconditional love demands so many of the qualities we have discussed throughout this book, such as passion, receptivity, and self-transcendence. This is because of the powerful link between unconditional love and creativity.

Artists love their art regardless of where it leads them. We have seen that the artist's path is rarely an easy one. This is why the hero's journey is such a fitting metaphor for the creative adventure. To create means to take bold leaps into the unknown. What else could inspire such abandon? We already know that love is a driving force in Deep Creativity, but we may not have realized how complete that love must be.

When our relationship with the Creator is grounded in unconditional love so that we identify the Creator as the Beloved, we are able to see the Beloved in all things. How could we not? And we undergo a transformation that makes creativity inevitable. We grasp that we are creating everything that penetrates our awareness—absolutely everything. Unconditional love lets us assume our rightful place in the universe as creative agents, giving us the power to become anything by being aware of it, and creating it by becoming it. Once we have crossed the threshold of unconditional love, this type of creativity begins to happen as effortlessly as waking up in the morning.

## The Eye of God

Our book cover features the Helix Nebula, also known as the Eye of God. In 2003, NASA released images of this nebula taken by the Hubble Space Telescope. I never saw any of the NASA photos until many years later, but by then I was already quite familiar with the image. The reason is that I have been seeing it when I close my eyes. This has been a regular occurrence for me since 2014.

To me, the Eye of God is the creative trinity: Creator-creating-creation. The actual nebula consists of ionized gases and dust, illuminated by high-energy radiation. What I see is almost identical in appearance. At the center is the alternating light and darkness of pure consciousness, giving way to the intricate forms corresponding to the universal mind, and engulfed by the radiance of love and joy. The fact that the same basic pattern occurs at a cosmic level and in my mind's eye should not be surprising. It attests to the fractal nature of the universal mind.

The Eye of God began appearing to me on a regular basis when I started opening myself up to the power of unconditional love. This is not surprising. I wanted to direct my unconditional love to the Creator and all that it encompasses.

Why not? If I am going to do anything, I want to do it all the way. Unconditional love for a friend, a family member or a pet is wonderful. But I wanted to know what would happen if I were to extend my love as far as it would go. That is when I started seeing the Eye of God.

When the image appears, it sends me into ecstasy. At those moments, I feel myself merging into the Creator, but I also feel the entire universe doing the same. Then the creation cycle begins unfolding inside of me. The whole universe emerges from pure consciousness and merges back into it, propelled by love and joy. I can feel the formless unity of the Creator shattering into a billion pieces and then coming back together again, so constantly and repeatedly that I surrender to what feels like spasms of breath or gentle laughter. It is a steady pulsation that takes over my entire body.

When the Eye of God comes to me, it is far from static. The emerging phase of the creation cycle appears as an expansion from the center of the image, and the merging phase looks like a contraction. All of this is going on at the same time. Picture a torus like the one shown here:

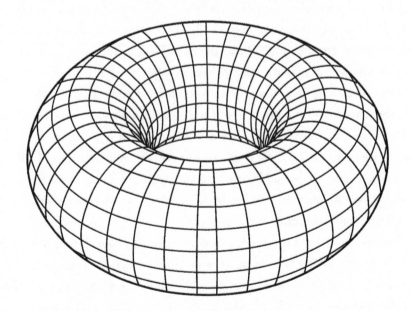

A torus seen from the side

Imagine that the outer surface of the torus is radiating out from the center and then enfolding back into itself. If you were looking at the torus from above, you might only see the outward motion—the opposite motion would be taking place on the underside of the image, outside of your view. This is how the Eye of God appears to me.

When I experience this image in my mind's eye, the act of creating becomes easy for me. In fact, it is almost inevitable. I gain access to insights and perspectives that had not been available to me previously. All of creation is being revealed to me in an instant, and I try to grasp whatever I can of it. My attention acts as a bottleneck that limits what I can absorb from the experience. But most of my understanding of Deep Creativity has come in this way.

Nothing changes in the creative process but the contents of our minds. We simply gain access to what has been there all along. Creativity is ultimately a matter of reaching beyond our self-imposed limits. Much like the imaginary "box" that many of us construct when trying to solve the nine-dot problem, these limits are arbitrary and artificial. We may convince ourselves that they are real—and even absolute—but the story of humanity tells us otherwise. Throughout history, artists and mystics alike have been transcending these limits with impunity. For such individuals, the boundaries of the mind have about as much significance as national borders have to migratory birds.

Deep Creativity is a vision of our common destiny. Each of us has the capacity to transcend the limits of our individual minds so that we can be free to fly. We are all creative agents, but mostly we remain unaware of this reality. And so, we go about our daily lives, creating without full awareness of what we are doing, or more importantly, what we are capable of doing. With the proper intention, we can immerse ourselves in the creative experience in ways that reveal the splendor abiding within our own hearts.

As you know, I did not set out to write a how-to book. I simply intended to shine a light on an entire universe of possibilities that has been tucked away in a dark little corner of the human spirit. If you have read this far, it is because you already know the truths I have shared with you. These truths resonate deep within you, and now you may need to ask yourself an important question: *What do I do with this information?*

Maybe the answer is: Nothing. Maybe the answer is: Everything. This, of course, is entirely up to you. Deep Creativity is a matter of choice more than aptitude. It requires a bold leap, from the safe and familiar to the unknown. The only reason to make that leap is that you know there is something more for you, something greater. A magnificent adventure awaits. Here is the chance to go deeper into the mysterious essence of life, to discover your true nature, and to connect with ideas and possibilities far greater than anything you have yet to imagine.

Your reaction to this might be: *Hmm. That is all quite interesting. I will take it under advisement.* Then this book may have planted a seed that could sprout one day and grow into a majestic tree. But perhaps your heart is saying: *This is for me. Sign me up! How do I get started?* I have written this book with you in mind. And I conclude it by answering your question. Here is how you can get started on this path:

## Unconditional Love Invocation

Given that that the creative process is more of a circle than a straight line, it seems fitting to end this book at the beginning. The entire journey of Deep Creativity starts with unconditional love. This, more than anything, sets in motion the chain of events that propels us beyond the limits of our own minds and to the very source of all creation.

Unconditional love means merging completely with the Beloved. Who is the Beloved? It can be anyone or anything you choose. Once you have opened yourself up to unconditional love, the identity of the Beloved does not really matter. This is just your starting point.

Ultimately, you will find that unconditional love is limitless. It cannot be confined solely to a single entity. Just as there is only one consciousness, there is only one Beloved. Once you have experienced unconditional love, you will feel a connection with everyone and everything you encounter. But you have to start somewhere. This is why I have developed the Unconditional Love Invocation (ULI).

Before you do the invocation, envision the Beloved in the form of a specific person, pet, plant, place, or other entity. If you find it helpful to have a photograph or other memento on hand to help you focus, by all means do so. You will say the following words with the Beloved in mind. Each line appears in bold face, with an explanation of its significance directly below it:

### Lover and Beloved are one.

In love, there is no separation. The one that is aware and the one that abides in awareness are one. Love is the recognition of that oneness.

### I love you.

This most familiar of statements can have profound significance when said with total feeling. It declares to the world: "I am the Beloved seeing the Beloved in the Beloved."

### You, Beloved, you, there is only you.

There is and has only ever been one Beloved because there is only one consciousness. The lover sees through the illusion of separateness to recognize this fundamental fact. Here are two apparently different entities, and yet consciousness is the same within both. In fact, consciousness is the same everywhere we turn. To love unconditionally is to see the Beloved in all things.

### I give myself to you completely, Beloved, and receive you completely.

Beyond simply acknowledging the Beloved in another entity, we merge with the Beloved. Love inspires perfect generosity, allowing us to give ourselves completely to the Beloved, and perfect receptivity, allowing us to receive the Beloved completely. If there is only one consciousness, then this gesture may seem like an empty one. Are we not just giving ourselves to ourselves, and conversely receiving ourselves into ourselves? Yes, that is in fact the case, but until we do both, we are not fully aware of this identity.

### I am in you, Beloved, as you are in me.

Through perfect generosity, we cross the threshold of separateness and penetrate the Beloved, giving every bit of ourselves in love. And through perfect receptivity, we allow the Beloved to return the favor. The illusion of separateness ends here. We know that the Creator of the universe is both divisible and indivisible. That which can be divided can also be united. By merging with the Beloved, we realize this unification through the power of love.

### You and I are one.

When we love unconditionally, the veil of separateness falls away. We declare our oneness with the Beloved, but even this beautiful declaration cannot go far enough. At this moment, there is no "you" or "I." We can tell that the ULI has been effective when we experience something so profound and transcendent that words fail us. This declaration is simply the best we can do, even if it is less than adequate.

### And so it is.

An invocation works when it takes us from a declared intention to an actual experience. We conclude the ULI by acknowledging this shift. The next moment is one of silence, when we allow ourselves to feel the perfect communion we were able to invoke through our words and our actions.

The important thing, with respect to the ULI, is to do it wholeheartedly, with total feeling. It does not work unless you can feel it completely in your heart. When you say the ULI to someone or something with total feeling, it will transform you. When you say it to someone with total feeling *and* they say it back to you with total feeling, it will transform the world. Nothing is more profound than unconditional love shared between two people. This can unleash creative power in the most dramatic way imaginable.

When two people share unconditional love, they become one body, one heart, and one mind. To know if you are experiencing it, ask yourself this question: *Do I accept as my own everything about the Beloved?* This has to include everything the Beloved does, says, or thinks. Otherwise, you are not quite there yet. Just keep doing the invocation until it takes hold completely. And it will.

The invocation includes the words, "You, Beloved, you, there is only you." That is because the Beloved is the Creator. There is only one Beloved. That is all there has ever been or ever will be. The Beloved assumes myriad forms. When you can recognize the Beloved in even a single person, animal, plant, place, or treasured gift, you open the door. Eventually, you realize that you are speaking these words directly to the Creator.

That being the case, you might as well say the ULI with total feeling. Call the Creator by any name you like: God, Great Spirit, Divine Will, or anything else that resonates for you. This is really a matter of cultural upbringing and personal preference. What you are naming extends far beyond any label, category, or concept. So, it makes no difference how you address the Creator.

Deep Creativity begins here. Eventually, you will love the Creator so unconditionally that there is no separation. You will come to a profound realization: *The Creator and I are one.* Whatever the Creator can create, you will accept as your own. In so doing, you internalize the Creator. Everything we have been discussing can be found within you: the creative trinity, the creation cycle, consciousness and mind, thoughts and things, love and joy, ecstasy and bliss.

Do you doubt this is possible? Could the entire universe, as well as its source and essence, be abiding in you? Yes, of course it is. All of creation is unfolding at this very moment right inside of you. When you are fully present and fully engaged, you will know what a spectacular celebration this is. Your coming-out party is already in progress: the guests have arrived, the table has been set, and all the party favors are in place. The only thing missing is the guest of honor.

# ABOUT THE AUTHOR

Victor Shamas, Ph.D., has dedicated his life to understanding and exploring the experience of being fully alive (EBFA), as well as the sensations that give rise to it, including: passion, intuition, receptivity, playfulness, and self-transcendence. As a University of Arizona psychologist, he has studied the relationship of the EBFA with health, well-being, and creativity. For more than two decades, he has brought together and mentored free spirits who, like him, recognize the importance of the  EBFA as both a source of motivation and a guiding force in their lives.

The EBFA is a central theme in everything Dr. Shamas has written. *The Chanter's Guide* details the healing properties of the EBFA and explains how the practice of chanting can facilitate this kind of transformative experience. In *The Way of Play*, he explains how a variety of play activities can act as vehicle for EBFAs. *Repose: The Potent Pause*, co-authored with health psychologist Jhan Kold, introduces an effective tool that can induce an EBFA at no cost and with minimal effort or time commitment. In *Deep Creativity*, Dr. Shamas examines the central role of the EBFA in the creative act.

Dr. Shamas heads two groups that serve the needs of free spirits: PlayHaven, which offers creative play for people of all ages, and Global Chant, a network of chanting circles that embraces wisdom and sacred music from all traditions. The mission of both is to provide a venue and activities that attract free spirits and promote the EBFA. Dr. Shamas has spoken to groups in four continents on topics related to the EBFA, including creativity, play, Repose, chanting, self-transcendence and the future of spirituality.

Putting his ideas about creativity into practice, Dr. Shamas has written several hundred musical compositions; produced over 200 instructional videos; developed and taught 25 university courses in psychology; organized a global event called WAVE1 that involved approximately one million participants in 40 countries; recorded three music CDs; designed multimedia materials on the neuroscience of addiction; invented an automated solar water distiller; created an anti-inflammatory health program, called Victor's Inflammation Mend (VIM), to lower the risk of chronic illness; and directed the Intuition in Pregnancy study, which has been featured in the national media, including *USA Today*, *Pregnancy* magazine, and NBC's *Today* show.

# The Ten Tenets of Deep Creativity

Tenet #1: Creativity is not what you think.

Tenet #2: All creating is becoming.

Tenet #3: Consciousness is the ultimate source of all creation, including human creativity.

Tenet #4: Creativity has two phases: merging and emerging.

Tenet #5: Creative energy takes two forms: joy is the energy of emerging, and love the energy of merging.

Tenet #6: The three elements of creativity are: Creator, creating, and creation.

Tenet #7: The creative process is a heroic adventure consisting of three stages: Departure, Initiation, and Return.

Tenet #8: The ultimate reward of creativity is the sheer joy of the Creator.

Tenet #9: Discovery learning and creating are one and the same.

Tenet #10: Only the contents of our minds change as the result of the creative process.

APPENDIX 2

# The Rediscovery of Consciousness

## Victor Shamas, Ph.D.

The scientific study of consciousness was founded on a misconception that has plagued the field for more than a century. The misconception is so pervasive and subtle that not a single psychologist, neuroscientist or philosopher has noted it. Yet, it serves only to limit the advancement of consciousness studies. The issue has to do with the confounding of two disparate notions: consciousness and cognition.

In his classic *Principles of Psychology*, William James laid the groundwork for consciousness studies (James, 1890). Chapter IX of *Principles*, entitled "The Stream of Thought," includes a discussion of the "five characters in thought" that are still accepted as the defining features of consciousness. But could it be that these five characteristics do not pertain to consciousness at all? Notice the title of the chapter. Clearly, James was referring to cognition and *not* consciousness. An important distinction must be made between the two.

Cognition, of course, is the set of mental processes that includes attention, perception, memory, language, learning, reasoning, problem-solving, and decision-making. The tendency to equate consciousness with conscious cognition can be traced to James himself, who wrote, "I use the word thinking, in accordance with what was said on p. 186, for every form of consciousness indiscriminately." Two years after "The Stream of Thought" appeared in print, he published a very similar chapter entitled, "The Stream of Consciousness" (James, 1892), demonstrating that he considered *thought* and *consciousness* to be interchangeable.

Yet, consciousness and conscious thought—or more precisely, conscious cognition—are distinct phenomena. To illustrate this, consider the pattern of findings known to cognitive neuropsychologists as a *double dissociation*. The classic example can be found in the work of Broca (1861), whose patients had intact speech production with impaired comprehension, and Wernicke (1875), whose patients showed the reciprocal pattern. The fact that each function—speech production and comprehension—can exist in the absence of the other suggests that the two are independent of one another and may involve different processing systems in the brain.

Similarly, a double dissociation can be observed with consciousness and cognition. There is extensive evidence that cognition takes place in the absence of consciousness, as can be seen in the vast research literature on implicit memory, subliminal perception, implicit learning, and related phenomena that are considered part of the "cognitive unconscious" (Kihlstrom, 1987). Conversely, the experience of consciousness in the absence of cognition is familiar to many of the estimated 20 million Americans who practice meditation. This experience has been corroborated in the reports and observations of adept meditators from every part of the world. Here is a typical example:

"Past thoughts had died away, the future had not yet arisen; the stream of my thoughts was cut right through. In that pure shock a gap opened, and in that gap was laid bare a sheer, immediate awareness of the present, one that was free of any clinging. It was simple, naked, and fundamental." (Rinpoche, 1994).

Establishing the functional independence of consciousness and cognition is critical to the advancement of consciousness studies. Perhaps we can learn something from Buddhist psychology, which relies on the following metaphor: Consciousness is the sky and cognition the clouds moving across it (e.g. Taeger, 1999). Although the sky itself is constant, the pattern of clouds that fills the sky can change from one moment to the next. This analogy makes it possible to distinguish between the medium of consciousness and the mental contents that occupy it.

With this distinction in mind, let us revisit the fiver higher-order characteristics of consciousness identified by William James:

1) *Subjectivity.* When James writes that "every thought tends to be part of a personal consciousness," he is clearly referring to cognition. The mental activity that occupies consciousness is indeed personal, as James points out in the following statement: "My thought belongs with my other thoughts, and your thought with your other thoughts." However, the medium of consciousness itself exists independently of all mental contents, including the concept of self. This precludes the notion of a "personal" consciousness. After all, how can consciousness belong to an "I" that does not exist? Consciousness cannot be subjective because it draws no distinction between subject and object.

2) *Change.* James states, "Within each personal consciousness thought is always changing." Again, it seems that James is confounding consciousness and cognition. Drawing upon the Buddhist analogy, the clouds that move across the sky may come and go, but the sky itself remains relatively constant. His claim that "no state once gone can recur and be identical with what it was before" is debatable. If only mental contents change from one moment to the next, then it is likely that consciousness in the absence of such contents is completely stable. "Like the empty sky it has no boundaries/Yet it is right here, ever serene and clear" (Yung-chia, cited in Rinpoche, 1994).

3) *Continuity.* "Within each personal consciousness thought is sensibly continuous," James writes. Yet he acknowledges the existence of temporal interruptions: "Even where there is a time-gap, the consciousness after it feels as if it belonged together with the consciousness before it, as another part of the same self." James is not referring to continuity but rather *coherence*, which is a characteristic of cognition. Although mental activity can be interrupted by sleep, the fact that individuals waking up in the morning still consider themselves to be the same person with the same identity and memories they had when they went to sleep the night before points to the fact that the mental contents before and after sleep are logically

consistent and thematically related. Any continuity experienced by the sleeper is illusory, given that the flow of thought was clearly disrupted by a period of sleep.

Cognition is coherent yet not continuous, whereas consciousness is exactly the opposite. Unlike waking mental activity, consciousness does not get disrupted by sleep. Clearly, individuals are conscious during REM (Aserinsky & Kleitman, 1953), and even when awakened from NREM, they often report some type of conscious experience (Herman, Ellman & Roffwarg, 1978). Although this experience may be distinct from the type of conscious cognition that takes place during waking, it supports the notion that consciousness is continuous.

When dissociated from cognition, consciousness lacks coherence simply because there are no mental contents to cohere. In the absence of mental activity, consciousness is undifferentiated, which means that there is no stream of thought requiring integration.

4) *Intentionality*. One of the more obscure meanings of the word, *intend*, is "to point to something." According to James, consciousness "always appears to deal with objects independent of itself." Once again, James is referring to "the cognitive function of thought" and specifically to the process of mental representation. In later works, he acknowledges that consciousness does not require such symbolic processes. "There are two ways of knowing things," James writes, "knowing them immediately or intuitively, and knowing them conceptually or representatively." Of these two ways of knowing, he adds, only the latter is characterized by intentionality. "To know immediately, then, or intuitively, is for mental content and object to be identical."

5) *Selectivity*. James is specifically describing the function of attention when observing, "It is interested in some parts of these objects to the exclusion of others, and welcomes or rejects—*chooses* from among them, in a word—all the while." Although the relationship between attention and consciousness continues to be a subject of debate, researchers generally agree that: a) the two are distinct; and b) attention is specifically a cognitive process. The selective function of attention is undeniable; it filters out irrelevant information and only allows the most important or salient thoughts into conscious cognition. "But we do far more than emphasize things, and unite some, and keep others apart," James observes. "We actually *ignore* most of the things before us."

When dissociated from cognition, consciousness does not require selectivity because there are no thoughts to emphasize or to ignore. According to Deikman (1973), consciousness can assume a receptive mode that involves "intake of the environment rather than manipulation." He argues that such receptivity is not necessarily passive: "'Letting it' is an activity, but a different activity than 'making it'."

The phenomenon of consciousness appears to be devoid of subjectivity, change, intentionality or selectivity, all of which are characteristic of cognition. On the other hand, consciousness possesses the quality of continuity that cognition lacks. Although cognition can be considered coherent, it is subject to disruption—as James himself acknowledged—which prevents it from being truly continuous. Moreover, consciousness and cognition are dissociable from an empirical standpoint. There is little doubt that the two phenomena are distinct. Even so, the field of consciousness studies has yet to acknowledge that fact.

As long as consciousness continues to be confounded with conscious cognition, consciousness researchers will continue to operate on the fringes of this phenomenon, making little progress in understanding basic human experiences such as creative inspiration or mystical union. Researchers have made great advances over the past three decades in comprehending the conditions under which consciousness is absent. Yet we continue to know so little about its presence.

# NOTES

## Introduction

1   *Riding Giants.* Directed by Stacy Peralta. Sony Pictures Classic. 2004.

2   Hennessey, Beth A., & Teresa M. Amabile. "Creativity." *Annual Review of Psychology* 61 (2010): 569-598.

3   The term "creative process" appears 17 times in the body of this 29-page review article: 12 times in a theoretical or speculative manner (e.g. "we must arrive at a far more detailed understanding of the creative process"), three times in reference to laboratory research with randomly selected subjects, and twice describing research on group creativity done in an organizational (i.e. corporate) setting. None of the research cited in the article draws upon the expertise of artists immersed in the creative process on a daily basis.

4   Graham Wallas, *The Art of Thought* (New York: Harcourt, Brace, & World, 1926).

5   Tom Wolfe, *The Electric Kool-Aid Acid Test* (New York: Bantam Books, 1968), p. 39.

6   My first publication was a chapter entitled "Hypnosis and Creativity," co-authored with legendary hypnosis researcher Patricia Bowers, which appeared in *Contemporary Hypnosis Research*, by Erika Fromm and Michael R. Nash (New York: Guilford Press, 1992).

7    Victor A. Shames, "Is There Such a Thing as Implicit Problem-Solving?" Ph.D. diss., University of Arizona, 1994, http://socrates.berkeley.edu/~kihlstrm/PDFfiles/VICTOR_PHD.pdf.

8    Victor A. Shamas and Jhan T. Kold, *Repose: The Potent Pause* (Tucson, AZ: Create Space, 2015).

## Chapter 1

9    Robert Henri, *The Art Spirit*. (New York: Basic Books, 1923), p. 159.

10    Gary E. Schwartz, *The G. O. D. Experiments: How Science is Discovering God in Everything, Including Us* (New York: Atria Books, 2006), p. 281.

11    Bruce L. Miller, Kyle Boone, Jeffrey L. Cummings, Stephen L. Read, and Fred Mishkin. "Functional correlates of musical and verbal ability in frontotemporal dementia." *British Journal of Psychiatry* 176 (2000): 458-463.

12    Peter I. Tchaikovsky, *The Life and Letters of Peter Ilich Tchaikovsky* (London: Bodley Head, 1906), pp. 311-312.

13    Donna W. La Cour, ed. *Artists in Quotation: A Dictionary of the Creative Thoughts of Painters, Sculptors, Designers, Writers, Educators, and Others* (Jefferson, NC: McFarland, 1989), p. 88.

## Chapter 2

14    John Rewald, *Post-Impressionism, from Van Gogh to Gauguin* (New York: Museum of Modern Art, 1956), p. 86.

15    Warren Roberts and Harry T. Moore, eds. *Phoenix II: Uncollected, Unpublished, and Other Prose Works by D. H. Lawrence* (New York: Viking Press, 1968), p. 605.

16    Mark Hertsgaard, *A Day in the Life: The Music and Artistry of the Beatles* (New York: Delta Trade Paperbacks, 1995), pp. 118-119.

17    Arthur M. Abell, *Talks with Great Composers* (New York: Philosophical Library, 1955), p. 137.

18    Ken Wilber, ed. *Quantum Questions: Mystical Writings of the World's Great Physicists* (Boston: Shambhala, 2001), p. 81.

19    Robert Sluss (entomologist) in discussion with the author, April 1985.

20   Lee Hall, *Betty Parsons: Artist, Dealer, Collector* (New York: H. N. Abrams, 1991), p. 28.

21   Donna W. La Cour, ed. *Artists in Quotation: A Dictionary of the Creative Thoughts of Painters, Sculptors, Designers, Writers, Educators, and Others* (Jefferson, NC: McFarland, 1989) p. 161.

22   Mark E. Koltko-Rivera, M. E. "Rediscovering the later version of Maslow's hierarchy of needs: Self-transcendence and opportunities for theory, research, and unification." *Review of General Psychology* 10 (2006): 302-317.

23   Wassily Kandinsky, *Concerning the Spiritual in Art*. (Berlin: Der Sturm, 1912), p. 43.

24   Larry Chang, ed. *Wisdom for the Soul: Five Millennia of Prescriptions for Spiritual Healing* (Washington, DC: Gnosophia, 2006), p. 385.

# Chapter 3

25   Will Grohmann, *Wassily Kandinsky: Life and Work* (New York: H. N. Abrams, 1958), p. 64.

26   Gary E. Schwartz, *The G. O. D. Experiments: How Science is Discovering God in Everything, Including Us* (New York: Atria Books, 2006), p. 281.

27   Mark Hertsgaard, *A Day in the Life: The Music and Artistry of the Beatles* (New York: Delta Trade Paperbacks, 1995), pp. 118-119.

28   William James, *Principles of Psychology* (New York: Henry Holt, 1890), p. 163.

29   Henry W. Longfellow, "Michael Angelo." *The Poetical Works of Henry Wadsworth Longfellow in Six Volumes: Volume VI* (Boston: Houghton, Mifflin, 1886), p. 65.

30   Arthur M. Abell, *Talks with Great Composers* (New York: Philosophical Library, 1955), p 120.

31   Ibid., 117.

32   Mark Hertsgaard, *A Day in the Life: The Music and Artistry of the Beatles* (New York: Delta Trade Paperbacks, 1995), p. 118.

33   Ibid.

34   Willis Harman and Howard Rheingold, *Higher Creativity: Liberating the Unconscious for Breakthrough Insights* (New York: G. P. Putnam's Sons, 1984), pp. 23-24.

35   Ibid.

36   Donna W. La Cour, ed. *Artists in Quotation: A Dictionary of the Creative Thoughts of Painters, Sculptors, Designers, Writers, Educators, and Others* (Jefferson, NC: McFarland, 1989), p. 90.

## Chapter 4

37   Andrew Harvey, ed. *The Essential Mystics: The Soul's Journey into Truth* (Edison, NJ: Castle Books, 1996), pp. 38-39.

38   "Creation Hymn." *Rig Veda*, Book 10, Hymn 129.

39   Ananda Coomaraswamy and I. B. Horner, *The Living Thoughts of Gotama the Buddha* (Mineola, NY: Dover Publications, 2000), p. 218.

40   David Bohm, *Wholeness and the Implicate Order* (London: Ark, 1988), p. 33.

41   Sogyal Rinpoche, *The Tibetan Book of Living and Dying* (San Francisco: Harper San Francisco, 1993), p. 350.

42   Jeff Wilson and Tomoe Moriya, eds. *Selected Works of D. T. Suzuki, Vol. III: Comparative Religion* (Oakland, CA: University of California Press, 2016), p. 170.

43   Donna W. La Cour, ed. *Artists in Quotation: A Dictionary of the Creative Thoughts of Painters, Sculptors, Designers, Writers, Educators, and Others* (Jefferson, NC: McFarland, 1989), p. 139.

44   Wallace Fowlie, trans. *Rimbaud, Complete Works, Selected Letters* (Chicago: University of Chicago Press, 1966), pp. 302-310.

45   D. H. Lawrence, "New Heaven and Earth." *D.H. Lawrence: Stories, Essays and Poems* (Worthing, UK: Littlehampton Book Services, 1969), p. 269.

46   Albert Einstein, *The World as I See It* (New York: Philosophical Library, 1949), p. 5.

47   Andrew Harvey, ed. *The Essential Mystics: The Soul's Journey into Truth* (Edison, NJ: Castle Books, 1996), p. 14.

48   Ibid., 18.

49  Ibid., 54.

50  Ibid., 139.

51  Ibid., 180.

52  Daniel C. Matt, ed. *The Essential Kabbalah: The Heart of Jewish Mysticism* (Edison, NJ: Castle Books, 1995), p. 26.

## Chapter 5

53  *Matthew* 5:44

54  Although the origin of the quote has never been substantiated, most sources attribute it to Davis. For an interesting discussion of this quote and its possible origin, please see Sally Chivers' essay, "No Place for Sissies: Gender, Age, and Disability in Hollywood," in *The Routledge Companion to Cinema and Gender*, edited by Kristin L. Hole, Dijana Jelača, E. Ann Kaplan, and Patrice Petro (London: Routledge, 2017).

55  Carl G. Jung, *Two Essays on Analytical Psychology* (London: Routledge, 1966), p. 74.

56  Joseph Campbell, *The Hero with a Thousand Faces* (Princeton, NJ: Princeton University Press, 1949), p. 257.

57  Sogyal Rinpoche, *The Tibetan Book of Living and Dying* (San Francisco: Harper San Francisco, 1993), p. 42.

58  Joseph Campbell, *The Hero with a Thousand Faces* (Princeton, NJ: Princeton University Press, 1949), p. 266.

## Chapter 6

59  Donna W. La Cour, ed. *Artists in Quotation: A Dictionary of the Creative Thoughts of Painters, Sculptors, Designers, Writers, Educators, and Others* (Jefferson, NC: McFarland, 1989), p. 57.

60  Ibid., 88.

61  Ibid., 82.

62  Malcolm Gladwell, *Outliers* (New York: Little, Brown and Co, 2008).

63  Stillman Drake, trans. *Discoveries and Opinions of Galileo* (New York: Anchor Books, 1957), p. 59.

64   Fran Parker and Stephen J. Parker, *Russia on Canvas: Ilya Repin* (State College, PA: Pennsylvania State University Press, 1980), p. 134.

65   Andrew Harvey, ed. *The Essential Mystics: The Soul's Journey into Truth* (Edison, NJ: Castle Books, 1996), p. 37.

66   Anna M. Cox, *Dharma Friends: No One Abandoned, No One Forgotten, No One Discarded* (Bloomington, IN: Xlibris, 2002), p. 20.

67   Donna W. La Cour, ed. *Artists in Quotation: A Dictionary of the Creative Thoughts of Painters, Sculptors, Designers, Writers, Educators, and Others* (Jefferson, NC: McFarland, 1989), p. 10.

68   Jon Krakauer, *Into the Wild* (New York: Villard, 1996), p. 18.

69   William Wordsworth, "Lines Composed a Few Miles above Tintern Abbey, on Revisiting the Banks of the Wye during a Tour. July 13, 1798." *The Complete Poetical Works of William Wordsworth* (London: Macmillan, 1888), p. 158.

70   Albert Einstein and Alice Calaprice, *The Ultimate Quotable Einstein* (Princeton, NJ: Princeton University Press, 2011), p. 99.

71   William B. Yeats, *Ideas of Good and Evil* (London: A. H. Bullen, 1903), p. 261.

72   Rollo May, *The Courage to Create* (New York: Norton, 1975), p. 123.

73   Rollo May, *Man's Search for Himself* (New York: Norton, 1953), p. 67.

74   Emanuel Swedenborg, *Conjugial Love and its Chaste Delights* (New York: American Swedenborg Printing and Publishing Society, 1871), p. 380.

75   *Matthew* 10:40

76   François de La Rochefoucauld, *The Moral Maxims and Reflections of the Duke de la Rochefoucauld* (London: Methuen and Co, 1912), p. 169.

77   Mihaly Czikszentmihalyi, *Flow: The Psychology of Optimal Experience* (New York: Harper Perennial, 1990).

78   *English Oxford Living Dictionaries*, accessed February 1, 2017, http://en.oxforddictionaries.com.

79   Andrew Harvey, ed. *The Essential Mystics: The Soul's Journey into Truth* (Edison, NJ: Castle Books, 1996), p. 38.

80   Rollo May, *The Courage to Create* (New York: Norton, 1975), p. 123.

# Chapter 7

81    Andrew Harvey, *The Essential Mystics: The Soul's Journey into Truth* (Edison, NJ: Castle Books, 1996), p. 148.

82    Albert Einstein, *The World as I See It* (New York: Philosophical Library, 1949), p. 26.

83    Colin M. Turbayne, ed. *Berkeley: Principles of Human Knowledge, Text and Critical Essays* (Indianapolis: Bobbs-Merrill, 1970), p. 313.

84    Andrew Harvey, *The Essential Mystics: The Soul's Journey into Truth* (Edison, NJ: Castle Books, 1996), p. 155.

85    Sogyal Rinpoche, *The Tibetan Book of Living and Dying* (San Francisco: Harper San Francisco, 1993), p. 349.

# Chapter 8

86    Lucinda Vardey, ed. *God in All Worlds: An Anthology of Contemporary Spiritual Writing* (New York: Pantheon Books, 1995), pp. 472-473.

87    Joseph Campbell and Bill Moyers, *The Power of Myth* (New York: Doubleday, 1988), p. 123.

88    Ibid., 156.

89    Ibid., 163.

90    Joseph Campbell, *The Hero with a Thousand Faces* (Princeton, NJ: Princeton University Press, 1949), p. 14.

91    Joseph Campbell and Bill Moyers, *The Power of Myth* (New York: Doubleday, 1988), p. 136.

92    Joseph Campbell, *The Hero with a Thousand Faces* (Princeton, NJ: Princeton University Press, 1949), p. 14.

93    Donna W. La Cour, ed. *Artists in Quotation: A Dictionary of the Creative Thoughts of Painters, Sculptors, Designers, Writers, Educators, and Others* (Jefferson, NC: McFarland, 1989), pp. 13-14.

94    James Egan, ed. (2015). *3000 Astounding Quotes*. Raleigh, NC: Lulu, 2015), p. 221.

95    Donna W. La Cour, ed. *Artists in Quotation: A Dictionary of the Creative Thoughts of Painters, Sculptors, Designers, Writers, Educators, and Others* (Jefferson, NC: McFarland, 1989), p. 14.

96  W. Somerset Maugham, *The Summing Up* (London: Heinemann, 1938), p. 310.

97  Henry Miller, *Stand Still Like the Hummingbird* (Norfolk, CT: New Directions, 1962), p. 60.

98  Joseph Campbell, *The Hero with a Thousand Faces* (Princeton, NJ: Princeton University Press, 1949), p. 30.

## Chapter 9

99 Joseph Campbell, *The Hero with a Thousand Faces* (Princeton, NJ: Princeton University Press, 1949), p. 78.

100 Ibid., 58.

101 Ibid., 71.

102 Ibid., 72.

103 Ibid., 40.

104 Ibid., 40-41.

105 Joseph Campbell and Bill Moyers, *The Power of Myth* (New York: Doubleday, 1988), p. 120.

106 Mark Hertsgaard, *A Day in the Life: The Music and Artistry of the Beatles* (New York: Delta Trade Paperbacks, 1995), p. 19.

107 Hunter Davies, *The Beatles* (New York: Norton, 1988), p. 31.

108 Callum McVickers, *Anxiety Antidotes: A Young Person's Pocket Guide to Conquering Worry* (United Kingdom: AnxietyAntidotes.net, 2015).

109 Laurie Carlson, *Thomas Edison for Kids: His Life and Ideas* (Chicago: Chicago Review Press, 2006), p. 122.

110 Andreas Moritz, *Lifting the Veil of Duality: Your Guide to Living without Judgment* (Brevard, NC: Ener-Chi Wellness Press, 2005), p. 238.

111 Jose Kaimlett, *Insights: Compilation of 200 Stories on the Insights of Life* (Berlin: Verlag GD Publishing, 2011), p. 87.

112 Joseph Campbell, *The Hero with a Thousand Faces* (Princeton, NJ: Princeton University Press, 1949), p. 59.

113 Loudon Wainwright III, "The Man who Wouldn't Cry" in *Attempted Mustache*, Columbia Records, 1973.

114 *Proverbs*, 1:24.

115 *Matthew* 22:14

116 Lao Tzu. *Tao Te Ching,* Chapter 64.

117 Joseph Campbell and Bill Moyers, *The Power of Myth* (New York: Doubleday, 1988), p. 120.

118 Gary E. Schwartz, *The G. O. D. Experiments: How Science is Discovering God in Everything, Including Us* (New York: Atria Books, 2006), p. 281.

119 Donna W. La Cour, ed. *Artists in Quotation: A Dictionary of the Creative Thoughts of Painters, Sculptors, Designers, Writers, Educators, and Others* (Jefferson, NC: McFarland, 1989), p. 95.

120 Sogyal Rinpoche, *The Tibetan Book of Living and Dying* (San Francisco: Harper San Francisco, 1993), p. 134.

121 Ibid.

122 Harry Chapin, "Taxi," in *Heads and Tales*, Elektra Records, 1972.

# Chapter 10

123 Joseph Campbell, *The Hero with a Thousand Faces* (Princeton, NJ: Princeton University Press, 1949), p. 97.

124 Ibid., 101.

125 Ibid., 121.

126 Ibid., 190.

127 Ibid., 217

128 Ibid., 172-192.

129 Ibid., 97-109.

130 Lucinda Vardey, ed. *God in All Worlds: An Anthology of Contemporary Spiritual Writing* (New York: Pantheon Books, 1995), p. 215.

131 Victor Shamas, *The Chanter's Guide: Sacred Chanting as a Shamanic Practice* (Tucson, AZ: Act on Wisdom, 2007), p. 154.

132 Ibid.

133 Joseph Campbell, *The Hero with a Thousand Faces* (Princeton, NJ: Princeton University Press, 1949), p. 91.

134 Mark Hitchcock, *Visits to Heaven and Back: Are They Real?* (Carol Stream, IL: Tyndale House, 2015), p. 69.

135 Donna W. La Cour, ed. *Artists in Quotation: A Dictionary of the Creative Thoughts of Painters, Sculptors, Designers, Writers, Educators, and Others* (Jefferson, NC: McFarland, 1989), p. 21.

136 Marcel Danesi, "The Original 'Thinking Outside the Box' Puzzle," *Psychology Today*. Posted March 06, 2009, https://www.psychologytoday.com/blog/brain-workout/200903/the-original-thinking-outside-the-box-puzzle.

137 Joseph Campbell, *The Hero with a Thousand Faces* (Princeton, NJ: Princeton University Press, 1949), p. 111.

138 Ibid., 114.

139 Isadora Duncan, *My Life* (New York: Horace Liveright, 1927), p. 2.

140 Donna La Cour, ed. *Artists in Quotation: A Dictionary of the Creative Thoughts of Painters, Sculptors, Designers, Writers, Educators, and Others* (Jefferson, NC: McFarland, 1989), p. 4.

141 Steve Jobs, Stanford commencement address (June 12, 2005).

142 Genevieve Stebbins, *Delsarte System of Expression* (New York: E. S. Werner, p. 23).

143 Joseph Campbell, *The Hero with a Thousand Faces* (Princeton, NJ: Princeton University Press, 1949), p. 128.

144 Ibid., 145.

145 Ibid., 147.

146 Abraham Maslow, *New Knowledge in Human Values* (New York: Harper and Row, 1959), p. 155.

147 Joseph Campbell, *The Hero with a Thousand Faces* (Princeton, NJ: Princeton University Press, 1949), p. 167.

148 *Dhammapada*, Verse 2.

149 Donna La Cour, ed. *Artists in Quotation: A Dictionary of the Creative Thoughts of Painters, Sculptors, Designers, Writers, Educators, and Others* (Jefferson, NC: McFarland, 1989), p. 145.

150 Joseph Campbell, *The Hero with a Thousand Faces* (Princeton, NJ: Princeton University Press, 1949), p. 182.

# Chapter 11

151 Joseph Campbell, *The Hero with a Thousand Faces* (Princeton, NJ: Princeton University Press, 1949), p. 20.

152 Ibid.

153 Ibid., 38.

154 Ibid., 54.

155 Ibid., 20.

156 Ibid., 207.

157 Ibid., 196-197.

158 Ibid., 207

159 Ibid., 218.

160 Ibid.

161 Ibid., 217

162 Thomas Wolfe, *You Can't Go Home Again* (New York: Harper and Bros, 1940).

163 Joseph Campbell, *The Hero with a Thousand Faces* (Princeton, NJ: Princeton University Press, 1949), p. 266.

164 Frederic C. Bartlett, *Remembering* (Cambridge, UK: Cambridge University Press, 1932).

165 Willis Harman, and Howard Rheingold, *Higher Creativity: Liberating the Unconscious for Breakthrough Insights* (New York: G. P. Putnam's Sons, 1984), pp. 35-36.

166 Ibid.

167 Carl Sagan, *Contact* (New York: Simon and Schuster, 1985).

168 Joseph Campbell, *The Hero with a Thousand Faces* (Princeton, NJ: Princeton University Press, 1949), p 218.

169 Donna La Cour, ed. *Artists in Quotation: A Dictionary of the Creative Thoughts of Painters, Sculptors, Designers, Writers, Educators, and Others* (Jefferson, NC: McFarland, 1989), p. 136.

170 Henry Miller, *Sunday after the War* (Norfolk, CT: New Directions, 1944), p. 14.

171 Joseph Campbell, *The Hero with a Thousand Faces* (Princeton, NJ: Princeton University Press, 1949), p. 36.

172 Ibid., 36-37.

173 Thomas H. Benton, *An Artist in America* (Columbia, MO: University of Missouri Press, 1937), p. 45.

174 Joseph Campbell, *The Hero with a Thousand Faces* (Princeton, NJ: Princeton University Press, 1949), p 37.

175 Jill Harness, "Six Famous Misquotes and Where they Came From," *Neatorama*, posted July 12, 2012, http://www.neatorama.com/2012/07/12/6-famous-misquotes-where-they-came-from/.

176 James E. Lindsay, *Daily Life in the Medieval Islamic World* (Westport, CT: Greenwood,2005), p. 27.

177 Baha'u'llah. *Writings on the Civilizing of Human Character*, accessed February 1, 2017, http://www.bahaullah.com/bahaullah-writings-human-character-part1.html.

178 Joseph Campbell, *The Hero with a Thousand Faces* (Princeton, NJ: Princeton University Press, 1949), p. 234.

179 Ibid., 229.

180 Robert Gottlieb and Robert Kimball, eds. *Reading Lyrics* (New York: Pantheon, 2000), p. 43.

181 Swami Nirvedananda, "Fundamentals of Brahmanda." In *The Mystery of Creation* (Mumbai, India: Central Chinmaya Mission Trust, 1986), p. 40.

182 Ram Shankar Misra, *The Integral Advaitism of Sri Aurobindo* (New Delhi, India: Motilal Banarsidass Publishing, 1998), p. 187.

183 Swami Adiswarandanda, *Meditation and its Practices: A Definitive Guide to Techniques and Traditions of Meditation in Yoga and Vedanta* (Woodstock, VT: Sky Paths Publishing, 2003), p. xvii.

## Chapter 12

184 Lama Yeshe, *Introduction to Tantra: The Transformation of Desire* (Boston: Wisdom Publications, 1987), p. 64.

185 Ibid., 66.

186 Ibid., 61.

187 Eric G. Wilson, *My Business is to Create: Blake's Infinite Writing* (Iowa City, IA: University of Iowa Press, 2011), p. 68.

188 Henry Miller, *Sexus* (New York: Grove Press, 1949), p. 154.

189 B. Maria Kumar, *To Be or Not to Be Happy* (Bhopal, India: Indra Publishing House, 2015), p. 95.

190 George Hegel, *Lectures on the Philosophy of History, Part IV: The German World* (London: H. G. Bohn, 1857), p. 374.

191 H. L. Havell, trans. *Longinus: On the Sublime* (London: Macmillan and Company, 1890), p. 37.

192 Wei-Huan Chen, "Reading between the Notes: The Genius of Yo-Yo Ma," *JConline*, posted October 8, 2014, http://www.jconline.com/story/entertainment/music/2014/10/08/yo-yo-ma-purdue/16917373/.

193 Malcolm Gladwell, "Secrets of Success," *Radiolab* (July 26, 2010).

194 David Epstein, *The Sports Gene: Inside the Science of Extraordinary Athletic Performance* (New York: Penguin Books, 2013), p. 240.

195 Donna La Cour, ed. *Artists in Quotation: A Dictionary of the Creative Thoughts of Painters, Sculptors, Designers, Writers, Educators, and Others* (Jefferson, NC: McFarland, 1989), p. 169.

196 Jason Evert, *Saint John Paul the Great: His Five Loves* (Lakewood, CO: Totus Tuus Press, 2014), p. 41.

197 John Cage, *Silence: Lectures and Writings* (Middletown, CT: Wesleyan University Press, 1961), p. 8.

198 Aaron Fisher, *The Way of Tea: Reflections on a Life with Tea* (North Clarendon, VT: Tuttle, 2010), p. 102.

199 National Sleep Foundation, "Lack of Sleep is Affecting Americans, Finds the National Sleep Foundation," accessed February 1, 2017, https://sleepfoundation.org/media-center/press-release/lack-sleep-affecting-americans-finds-the-national-sleep-foundation.

200 James McDermott, *The Writings of William James* (New York: Random House, 1968), p. 155.

201 Arthur J. Deikman, "Bimodal Consciousness," in *The Nature of Human Consciousness,* edited by Robert E. Ornstein (New York: Viking Press, 1973), p. 69.

202 Ibid., 71.

203 Rollo May, *The Courage to Create* (New York: Norton, 1975), p. 80.

204 Robert R. McCrae and Paul T. Costa, *Personality in Adulthood: A Five-Factor Theory Perspective* (New York: Guilford Press, 2003).

205 Sy Safransky, *Sunbeams: A Book of Quotations* (Chapel Hill, NC: Sun Publishing, 2012), p. 51.

206 Sheri Fink, "Quotes," *Goodreads*, Accessed February 1, 2017, https://www.goodreads.com/author/quotes/859191.Sheri_Fink

207 Jim Ballard, *Mind Like Water: Keeping your Balance in a Chaotic World* (Hoboken, NJ: Wiley & Sons, 2002), p. 82.

208 Alexander Shulgin, *PIHKAL: A Chemical Love Story* (Berkeley, CA: Transform Press, 1991), p. 7.

209 Wayne W. Dyer, *The Power of Intention: Learning to Co-create Your World Your Way* (Carlsbad, CA: Hay House, 2010), p.51.

210 Frederick Lenz, "Purity," *Rama Quotes*, Accessed February 1, 2017, http://www.ramaquotes.com/html/purity.html.

211 Graham Wallas, *The Art of Thought* (New York: Harcourt, Brace, & World, 1926).

212 Thich Nhat Hanh, *Bells of Mindfulness* (Berkeley, CA: Parallax Press, 2013), p. 77.

213 Michael Eigen, *Under the Totem: In Search of a Path* (London, UK: Karnac, 2016), p. 42.

214 Victor A. Shamas, V. A. & Jhan T. Kold, *Repose: The Potent Pause* (Tucson, AZ: Create Space, 2015), p. 12.

215 Ibid., 33-39.

216 Marianne Schnall, "Exclusive Interview with Zen Master Thich Nhat Hanh." *Huffington Post* (May 21, 2010), http://www.huffingtonpost.com/marianne-schnall/beliefs-buddhism-exclusiv_b_577541.html.

217 Victor A. Shamas and Jhan T. Kold, *Repose: The Potent Pause* (Tucson, AZ: Create Space, 2015), p. 59.

218 Anaïs Nin, *The Novel of the Future* (Athens, OH: Ohio University Press, 1968), p. 47.

219 Andre Geim, Nobel Banquet speech (December 10, 2010), https://www.nobelprize.org/nobel_prizes/physics/laureates/2010/geim-speech_en.html.

220 Joy Bennett Kinnon, "Gary Dourdan: More than a Sex Symbol," *Ebony Magazine* (September 2001), p. 10.

221 Lyle Lovett, "An Acceptable Level of Ecstasy (The Wedding Song)", in *Lyle Lovett*, MCA Records, 1986.

222 Bertrand Russell, *The Conquest of Happiness* (Philadelphia, PA: R. P. Pryne, 2015), p. 101.

223 Gustave Flaubert, *Madame Bovary* (New York: Brentano's, 1857), p. 136.

224 Henri Matisse, "Looking at Life with the Eyes of a Child," *New Outlook: A Digest of Ideas and Ideals* 9 (1956): 282.

225 Joseph Primm, *Live the Journey* (Eugene, OR: Resource Publications, 2010), p. 189.

226 The quote may be a misattribution, as pointed out in the *Wikiquote* entry for Dr. Seuss, accessed February 1, 2017, https://en.wikiquote.org/wiki/Dr._Seuss.

227 Immanuel Kant, *Grounding for the Metaphysics of Morals*, trans. J. W. Ellington (Indianapolis, IN: Hackett, 1993), p. 30.

228 Jeremy Sutton, *Painter IX Creativity: Digital Artist's Handbook* (Burlington, MA: Focal Press, 2013), p. 186.

229 *Matthew* 18:3

230 Clarissa Pinkola Estés, *Women who Run with the Wolves: Contacting the Power of the Wild Woman* (London, UK: Rider Books), p. 53.

231 Carl G. Jung, *Man in Search of a Soul* (New York: Routledge Classics, 1933), p. 67.

232 Simon Hattenstone, "Lady Gaga: Lording It." *The Guardian*, Posted May 13, 2011, https://www.theguardian.com/music/2011/may/14/lady-gaga-interview.

233 John Lennon, Yoko Ono, and David Sheff, *All We are Saying: The Last Major Interview with John Lennon and Yoko Ono* (New York: Griffin, 2000), p. 16.

234 Richard Garnett, *William Blake: Painter and Poet* (New York: Haskell House, 1971), p. 56.

235 William Blake, "Proverbs of Hell," Lines 8-9. *The Poetical Works of William Blake* (Oxford, UK: Oxford University Press, 1908).

236 Donna La Cour, ed. *Artists in Quotation: A Dictionary of the Creative Thoughts of Painters, Sculptors, Designers, Writers, Educators, and Others* (Jefferson, NC: McFarland, 1989), p. 164.

237 Harry Chapin, "Flowers are Red," in *Living Room Suite*, Elektra Records, 1978.

238 https://en.wikiquote.org/wiki/Jonathan_Swift

239 Sogyal Rinpoche, *The Tibetan Book of Living and Dying* (San Francisco: Harper San Francisco, 1993), p. 351.

240 Pamela H. MacKellar, *The Accidental Librarian* (Medford, NJ: Information Today, 2008), p. 75.

241 Agnes de Mille, *Martha: The Life and Work of Martha Graham* (New York: Random House, 1991), p. 264.

242 George Bernard Shaw, *Selected Plays with Prefaces, Vol. 2* (New York: Dodd, Mead, and Company, 1949), p. 7.

## Chapter 13

243 Linda Lee, Jack Vaughn, and Mike Lee, *The Bruce Lee Story* (Santa Clarita, CA: Ohara, 1989), p. 166.

244 Eren Sari, *Bruce Lee* (Antalya, Turkey: Nokta, 2016), p. 51.

245 Bruce Lee and John Little, *Striking Thoughts: Bruce Lee's Wisdom for Daily Living* (North Clarendon, VT: Tuttle, 2000), p. 13.

246 John Little, *The Warrior Within: The Philosophies of Bruce Lee* (New York: Chartwell, 2016), p. 121.

247 Paul Bowman, *Theorizing Bruce Lee: Film-Fantasy-Fighting-Philosophy* (New York: Rodopi, 2010), p. 101

248 Bruce Lee, *Tao of Jeet Kune Do* (Valencia, CA: Black Belt, 2011), p. 14.

249 Bruce Lee and John Little, *Striking Thoughts: Bruce Lee's Wisdom for Daily Living* (North Clarendon, VT: Tuttle, 2000), p. 105.

250 Ibid., 154.

251 Ferol N. Arcy and Patrick McDermott, *Mind Body Spirit: The Triangle of Life* (New York: iUniverse, 2007), p. 6.

252 Roy M. Pritchard. "Stabilized Images on the Retina." *Scientific American* 204 (1961): 72-78.

253 Bruce Lee and John Little, *Striking Thoughts: Bruce Lee's Wisdom for Daily Living* (North Clarendon, VT: Tuttle, 2000), p. 2.

254 Bruce Lee and John Little, *Bruce Lee: Artist of Life* (North Clarendon, VT: Tuttle, 1999), p. 121.

255 Linda Lee, Jack Vaughn, and Mike Lee, *The Bruce Lee Story* (Santa Clarita, CA: Ohara, 1989), p. 171.

256 Bruce Lee and John Little, *Striking Thoughts: Bruce Lee's Wisdom for Daily Living* (North Clarendon, VT: Tuttle, 2000), p. 19.

257 William James, *Principles of Psychology* (New York: Henry Holt, 1890), p. 488.

258 Lee and John Little, *Bruce Lee: Artist of Life* (North Clarendon, VT: Tuttle, 1999), p. 255.

259 Bruce Lee and John Little, *Striking Thoughts: Bruce Lee's Wisdom for Daily Living* (North Clarendon, VT: Tuttle, 2000), p. 31.

260 Ibid., 5.

261 Scott Winters, *Mind Unleashed: The God Within* (Lapeer, MI: Lulu, 2015), p. 57.

262 Bruce Lee and John Little, *Striking Thoughts: Bruce Lee's Wisdom for Daily Living* (North Clarendon, VT: Tuttle, 2000), p. 72.

263 Victor Shamas, *The Way of Play: Reclaiming Divine Fun and Celebration* (Tucson, AZ: Act on Wisdom, 2011), p. 18.

264 Cornelia Heinz, Heero Miketta, and Sascha Wagener, *The Missing Links of Martial Arts* (Manchester, UK: Lulu, 2014), p. 5.

265 Grateful Dead, "Truckin'," in *American Beauty*, Warner Bros. Records, 1970.

266 Bruce Lee and John Little, *Striking Thoughts: Bruce Lee's Wisdom for Daily Living* (North Clarendon, VT: Tuttle, 2000), p. 175.

267 Ibid., 178.

## Chapter 14

268 Larry Chang, ed. *Wisdom for the Soul: Five Millennia of Prescriptions for Spiritual Healing* (Washington, DC: Gnosophia, 2006), p. 605.

269 Stephen Mitchell, ed. *The Enlightened Mind: An Anthology of Sacred Prose* (New York: Harper Perennial, 1991), p. 67.

270 Ibid., 65.

271 William Blake, "Auguries of Innocence," in *Poets of the English Language*, edited by Wynstan Hugh Auden and Norman Holmes Pearson (New York: Viking Press, 1950), p. 18.

272 Stephen Mitchell, ed. *The Enlightened Mind: An Anthology of Sacred Prose* (New York: Harper Perennial, 1991), p. 102.

273 Amos Tversky (psychologist) in discussion with the author, February 1996.

274 Joseph Campbell, *The Hero with a Thousand Faces* (Princeton, NJ: Princeton University Press, 1949), p. 121.

275 Stephen Mitchell, ed. *The Enlightened Mind: An Anthology of Sacred Prose* (New York: Harper Perennial, 1991), p. 114.

276 Ibid., 112.

## Chapter 15

277 David Bohm and Mark Edwards, *Changing Consciousness: Exploring the Hidden Source of the Social, Political, and Environmental Crises Facing Our World*, (San Francisco: Harper San Francisco, 1991), p. 132.

278 The new field of positive psychology traces back to Martin Seligman's 1998 Presidential Address to the American Psychological Association, followed by this groundbreaking paper two years later: Martin E. P. Seligman and Mihaly Csikszentmihályi, "Positive Psychology: An Introduction." *American Psychologist* 55 (2000): 5-14.

279 Jeanne *Nakamura and Mihaly Csikszentmihályi, "Flow Theory and Research." In Handbook of Positive Psychology*, edited by *C. R. Snyder, Erik Wright, and Shane J. Lopez (New York: Oxford University Press, 2001), pp. 195–206.*

280 *Fearless*. Directed by Peter Weir. Warner Bros. 1993.

# Morgan James
# Speakers Group

www.TheMorganJamesSpeakersGroup.com

We connect Morgan James published
authors with live and online events
and audiences who will benefit
from their expertise.

CPSIA information can be obtained
at www.ICGtesting.com
Printed in the USA
BVOW09s1055051017
496819BV00001B/1/P

9 781683 505419